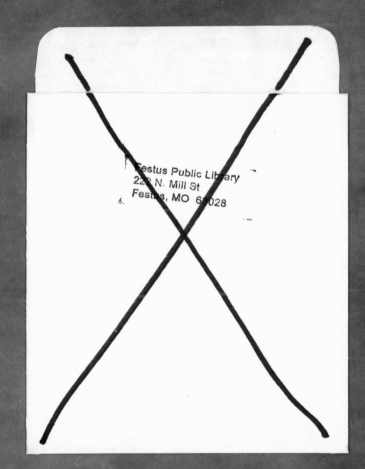

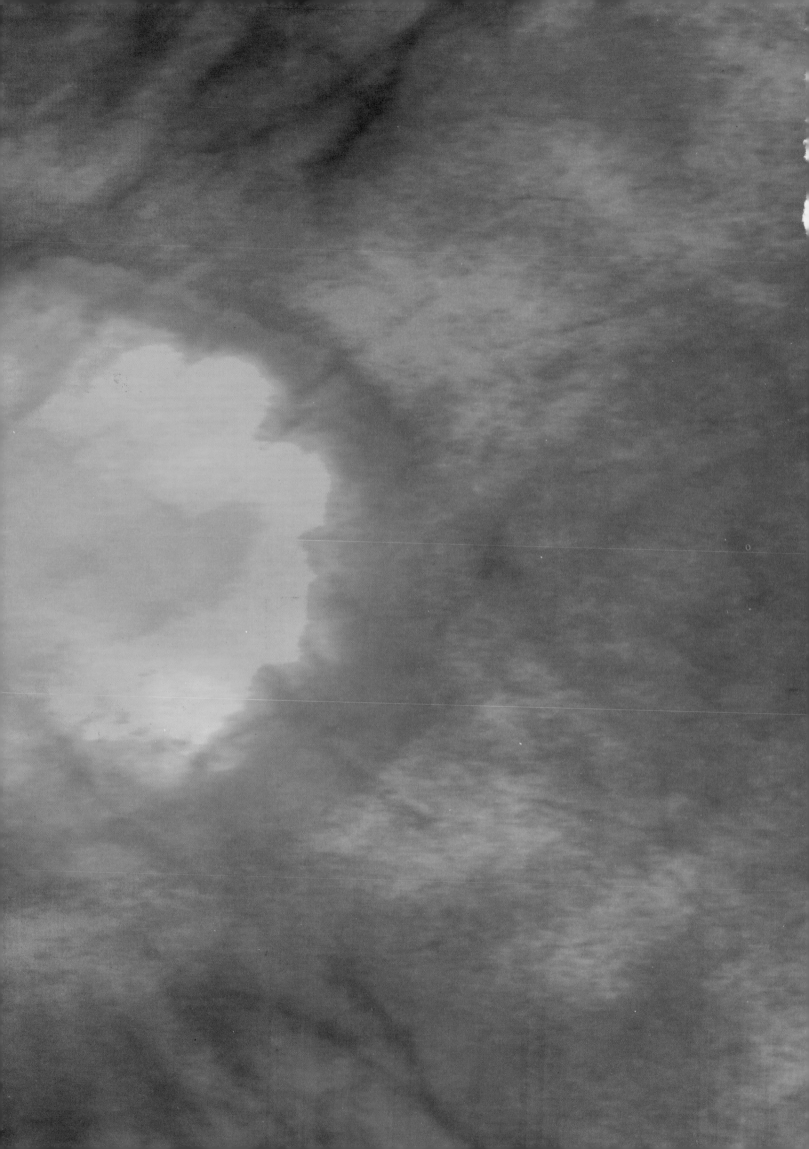

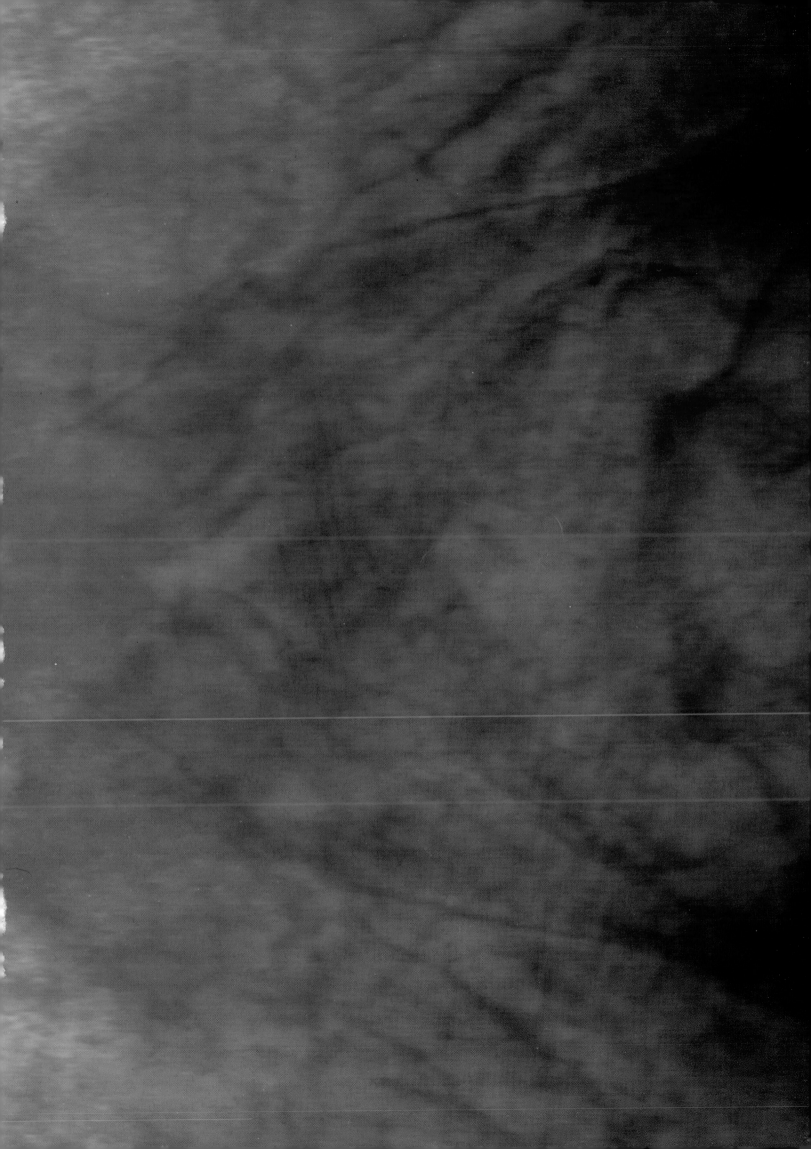

SACRED MYTHS:

Stories of World Religions

SACRED MYTHS:

Stories of
World Religions

Retold by

Marilyn McFarlane

SIBYL
Publications
Portland, Oregon

Published by Sibyl Publications, Inc.
600 S.E. Powell Blvd.
Portland, Oregon 97202
(503) 231-6519, 1-800-240-8566

ISBN 0-9638327-7-8

6 5 4 3 2 1

Consulting Editor: *Marge Columbus*

Graphic Design, Cover Design, and Illustrations: *Design Studio Selby:*
Brian Haselton, Matt Pinkerton, Egon Selby, Robert Selby, Jenifer Wilson

Calligraphy: *Cheryl Macy*

T36516

Story and illustration credits and permissions appear on page 100

Cataloging in Publication Data

McFarlane, Marilyn.
    Sacred myths : stories of world religions / retold by Marilyn
McFarlane.
        p. cm.
    Includes bibliographical references.
    SUMMARY: A sampling of the sacred stories of Buddhism,
Christianity, Hinduism, Islam, Judaism, and Native American and
other nature-based spiritual traditions.
    ISBN 0-9638327-7-8

    1. Mythology--Juvenile literature. 2. Religions--Juvenile
literature.   I. Title.

PZ8.1.M3437Sac 1996   291.1'3
                                       QBI96-20068

Printed and bound in Korea

To my grandchildren,
who love a good story

CONTENTS

T36516

ACKNOWLEDGMENTS

I owe thanks to a number of religious authorities and spiritual leaders who generously provided assistance and guidance in creating this book. Each person brings his or her own perspective to matters as close to the heart as religious beliefs. I have tried to make the stories accurate reflections of what I was told, but any errors to be found are mine alone.

Many thanks to Wajdi Said, Rabbi Emmanuel Rose, the Rev. William Creevey, Pritam Rohila, Swami Vishwa Premananda, Ani Paldron, Brooke Medicine Eagle, Lucinda Green, Sweet Medicine Nation, and Elinor Gadon.

For their comments and suggestions on the reading level of the text, I'm grateful to Chris Poole-Jones and Ginni Vick. Heartfelt thanks to Nan Narboe, Elaine Breshgold, and Dee Poth for their enthusiastic support and helpful criticism. My thanks to Wayne Ude and members of his Writing From Myth workshop for their perceptive observations.

I'm deeply thankful for the insight and encouragement of my husband, John Parkhurst. Finally, my thanks to the reader whose response meant the most: my grandson, Geoffrey Powell.

INTRODUCTION

Long ago, myths about gods and goddesses explained the natural world. When people heard thunder or saw lightning, they said the sky gods were angry; when the sun rose or rain fell on their fields or a rainbow appeared, they said the gods and goddesses made it happen. Religions formed around these powerful beings as people worshipped them, asked for their blessings, and expressed thanks.

Over the centuries religious beliefs changed and shifted, until now hundreds of different religions exist around the world, each with its own fervent followers. Some people think that their religion is the only true and correct one. Some have gone to war to force others to change their spiritual beliefs, because they want everyone to believe as they do. Why do they care so much, and why is religion so important?

Today science explains how nature and the universe work, and many people say that religion isn't needed anymore. Yet religious feelings and beliefs are as strong as ever. They must be more than a substitute for science.

What all the world's religions have in common is a belief in a greater power. Some of them have no word and no picture for this power; they say it's the force that makes the earth spin, the stars and planets move, and life grow and fade and grow again in a vast cycle. Others think of the power as a loving father or mother, and still others say it has many names and faces, male and female.

This book tells a few of the best-known stories of the main religions in the world today. Reading or hearing the stories will help you understand more about the beliefs and the people who base their lives on them.

These stories are called myths. Some might be considered fables or tales, but all are in the mythic tradition. To say a story is a myth does not mean it is a lie. It may not be literal fact, but it tells a story that is deeper than fact because it holds an important truth about life. We put the truth into story form because humans use stories and pictures to understand what cannot be seen and touched.

A myth is more than a tall tale, more than an adventure story. It shows us what is true about human beliefs.

THE GOLDEN RULE

BUDDHISM: HURT NOT OTHERS WITH THAT WHICH PAINS YOURSELF

CHRISTIANITY: DO UNTO OTHERS AS YOU WOULD HAVE THEM DO UNTO YOU

HINDUISM: TREAT OTHERS AS YOU WOULD YOURSELF BE TREATED

ISLAM: DO UNTO ALL MEN AS YOU WOULD WISH TO HAVE DONE UNTO YOU

JUDAISM: WHAT YOU YOURSELF HATE, DO TO NO MAN

NATIVE AMERICAN: LIVE IN HARMONY, FOR WE ARE ALL RELATED

SACRED EARTH: DO AS YOU WILL, AS LONG AS YOU HARM NO ONE

3

HURT NOT OTHERS WITH THAT WHICH PAINS YOURSELF

Budd

4

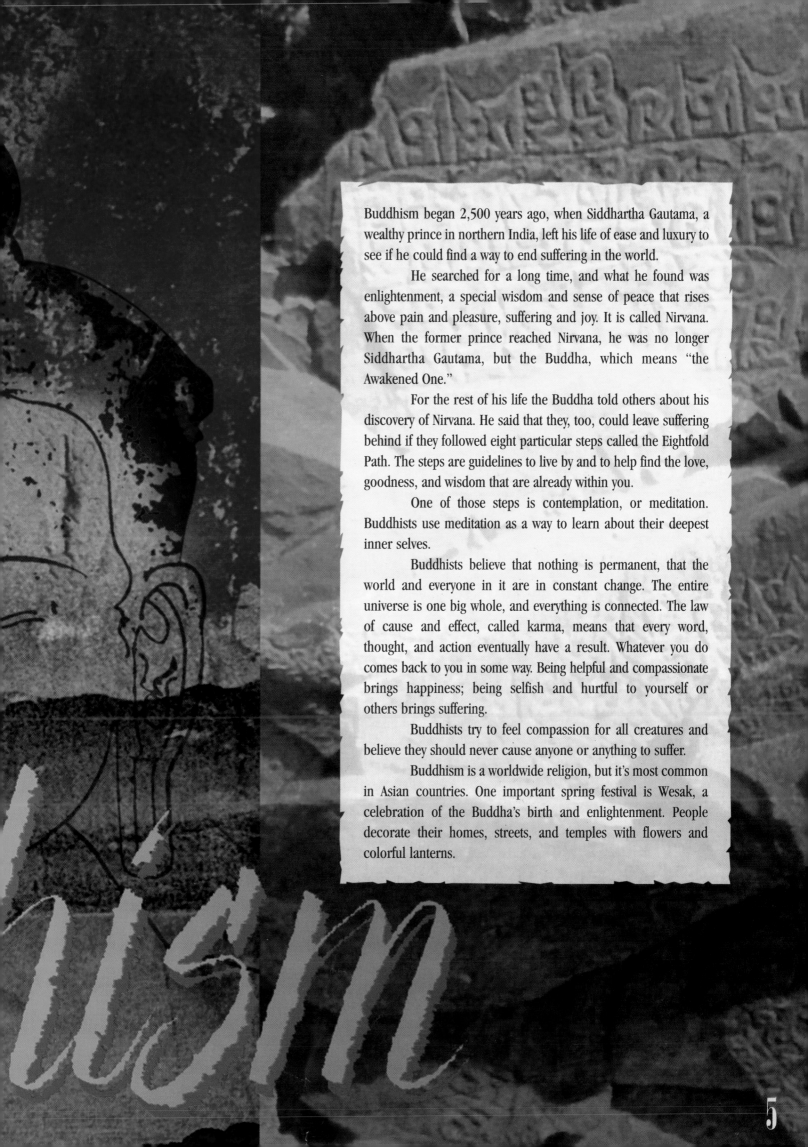

Buddhism began 2,500 years ago, when Siddhartha Gautama, a wealthy prince in northern India, left his life of ease and luxury to see if he could find a way to end suffering in the world.

He searched for a long time, and what he found was enlightenment, a special wisdom and sense of peace that rises above pain and pleasure, suffering and joy. It is called Nirvana. When the former prince reached Nirvana, he was no longer Siddhartha Gautama, but the Buddha, which means "the Awakened One."

For the rest of his life the Buddha told others about his discovery of Nirvana. He said that they, too, could leave suffering behind if they followed eight particular steps called the Eightfold Path. The steps are guidelines to live by and to help find the love, goodness, and wisdom that are already within you.

One of those steps is contemplation, or meditation. Buddhists use meditation as a way to learn about their deepest inner selves.

Buddhists believe that nothing is permanent, that the world and everyone in it are in constant change. The entire universe is one big whole, and everything is connected. The law of cause and effect, called karma, means that every word, thought, and action eventually have a result. Whatever you do comes back to you in some way. Being helpful and compassionate brings happiness; being selfish and hurtful to yourself or others brings suffering.

Buddhists try to feel compassion for all creatures and believe they should never cause anyone or anything to suffer.

Buddhism is a worldwide religion, but it's most common in Asian countries. One important spring festival is Wesak, a celebration of the Buddha's birth and enlightenment. People decorate their homes, streets, and temples with flowers and colorful lanterns.

The Birth Of The Buddha

In the glorious city of Kapilavastu, where the walls were encrusted with jewels and the gardens bloomed all year, there lived a wise and honest king named Suddhodana. His wife, Queen Maya, was as beautiful as a perfect lotus blossom, and she was as kind and good as her husband. The people in their kingdom lived in happiness.

One spring night, while Queen Maya lay sleeping on her perfumed couch high in the palace, she had a dream. She dreamed that a young white elephant with six tusks came to her from the sky, and with it were thousands of gods, all of them singing sweet songs of praise.

When Maya awoke, she felt a great joy that she could not explain. She rose from her bed and dressed in her brightest colors, and she glided down the stairs, out the high palace doors, and through the carved gates. She walked into the gardens to a shady grove of trees. There she sat on a bench and sent for the king to come to her.

When the king entered the grove, he took his wife's hand and asked, "Maya, why did you send for me?"

The queen answered, "I have had a strange dream, and I don't know what it means. I dreamed that a young white elephant with six tusks came to me, and thousands of gods sang my praises. Does this mean good or evil for us? Please call for a dream interpreter and ask him to tell us."

The king sent for the dream interpreter, who listened to the story with rapt attention. He said, "King Suddhodana and Queen Maya, this dream means that you have been supremely favored by the gods. You will have a son who will be rich in wisdom and praised by the world. Oh King, oh Queen, your son will be an enlightened one—a Buddha."

Suddhodana and Maya looked at each other with radiant eyes and felt a deep happiness and peace. The king called his servants. "This is a day to celebrate," he said. "Take money from the palace treasury and give it to the poor. Give food to the hungry, drink to the thirsty. See that every woman has flowers and perfume. Everywhere, sing songs of gratitude for the honor that has come to us."

Months went by, and one day Queen Maya knew it was time for her son to be born. She went to the king and said, "Today I will wander through the gardens. I want to hear the

birds singing, smell the fragrance of the flowers, and feel the soft air."

"But you should rest, my queen. Won't it tire you to walk those winding garden paths?"

"No, the innocent baby to come must be born among the flowers," Maya answered.

The king nodded. He turned to his servants and said, "Go to the gardens and deck the branches with hangings of silver and gold. When you carry the queen in her chair, wear necklaces of pearls and precious stones, and bring your flutes and harps so you can play melodies that will please the gods."

Bells rang as the palace gates opened. Peacocks spread their tail feathers and swans flew overhead while the queen passed by, seated on a chair carried by servants dressed in finery. In the gardens Queen Maya told the servants to set the chair on the ground. With her maidens she strolled among the flowers, stopping to sniff a perfect rose or watch a butterfly.

When she reached a certain tree that was covered with blossoms, she stopped. With a graceful hand she pulled a branch toward her and held it. She stood quite still, feeling

energy and power course through her, and in that moment a perfect child was born. The maidens near her lifted him in their arms and sang songs of praise. While the queen rested, they washed him in fresh water from the lotus pond and wrapped him in fine cloths.

The earth trembled, alive with delight. Buds burst into blossom, fruit ripened, the sky sang.

One of the servants hurried to tell the king. "My lord, your son is born!"

The king and his relations went to the garden where the baby lay in a soft bed of flowers. Birds sang in the trees, and harps and flutes played sweet music. King Suddhodana said, "His name is Siddhartha," and he and all the people bowed before the new prince.

One man raised his arms and said, "Prince Siddhartha will bring happiness to the world. We have been in darkness, but now we have light. This blessed child is the one who sees truth, and we will learn wisdom from him."

The baby, glowing with a golden light, smiled at all the people who had come to honor him.

The Buddha & The Bodhi Tree

Young Prince Siddhartha was raised in luxury. He lived in a palace where he slept on sheets of silk and ate the best of food. He was surrounded with flowers and music, love and laughter. The prince never knew that sadness or pain existed, because his father, King Suddhodana, kept his son well protected from them. When he grew up, however, the prince wanted to see the world that lay beyond the royal walls.

"No," declared his father. "Everything you could possibly want is right here. You have no need to leave the palace." Fearing that his beloved son would come to harm, he ordered the servants to lock the gates.

The prince did not argue, but he was even more curious. He searched until he found a way out of the palace, and he went into the city. There, as he traveled the streets, he was surprised to see sick people and beggars and people who were old and dying. It made him feel unspeakably sad.

"I didn't know these things existed. How can anyone be happy when they know they face old age and death?" he wondered. "What is the meaning of life? How do you find peace of mind?"

His head swirling with questions, the prince returned to the palace. He couldn't forget what he had seen. By now he was grown and had a wife and child, but his questions bothered him so much, Siddhartha finally decided that he had to leave his family and go into the world. There he would search for answers. And so, Siddhartha gave up all his rich clothing and jewels, said goodbye, and, no longer a prince, set out on his quest.

He searched for seven long, difficult years. For a time he joined a hermit who ate only fruit and leaves, dressed in rags, and walked barefoot on stony roads. Siddhartha went into the mountains, coming to the city to beg for food. He wandered in the forests with ascetics, men who tried to find wisdom by avoiding all pleasures and comforts. He gave up all food and shelter.

None of these gave him answers.

As he sat on a riverbank, thinking, he told himself, "Starvation does not lead to understanding and peace. I am becoming weak and gaining nothing. I must try another way."

The people who lived in a nearby village admired the holy man and brought him rice so he could grow strong again. Siddhartha found a cloth and from it made a simple garment to wear. He walked to the village.

A woman in the village was in her home, cooking rich, fresh milk with honey and rice, when she saw Siddhartha on her doorstep, surrounded by a dazzling light. In awe, she bowed. "Please honor me and enter my home," she said. Then she knelt, washed his dusty feet in sweet-scented water, and offered him a golden bowl full of the milk.

Siddhartha took it and thought, "The Buddhas of old, just before they attained supreme knowledge, were served a meal in a golden bowl. Maybe this bowl is a sign that the time has come for me to be a Buddha." He drank the milk, said goodbye to the woman, and walked to the river.

Night descended. Flowers closed, and birds called in

sleepy chirps. Stars glittered in the sky. Siddhartha continued on the path. He came to a pool where swans floated regally among white lotus flowers. At the far end of the pool was a tree—an immense tree, with spreading branches. Siddhartha knew it must be the Bodhi, the tree of knowledge.

He made a cushion of grass under the tree and sat on it, legs crossed, facing east. Then he said solemnly, "Until I have attained supreme knowledge, I shall not move from this seat."

The bright light that emanated from Siddhartha reached even into the deep realms where Mara, the Master of Illusions, the ruler of hope and fear, dwelled. The Master of Illusions snarled in anger. "Prince Siddhartha is seated under the tree of knowledge," he said to his servants. "He is concentrating his mind. If he finds peace and wisdom there, he will show others the way, and they will find Nirvana. The City of Illusions will be deserted. I will be a king without subjects, a leader without an army."

"No, no," cried the servants. "Gather your soldiers, strike him down while he sits under the Bodhi tree!"

Mara's army was a fearsome sight. Many of the soldiers had two or three heads, some had twenty arms. Their faces were hideous. Flames spewed from their eyes and blood from their mouths. Some had ears like goats, others like pigs or elephants. Around their necks they wore human fingers and jawbones.

With ear-splitting shrieks, the soldiers marched, bragging that they would soon crush the holy man.

First Mara tried to frighten Siddhartha with fierce gales of wind that uprooted trees and shook mountains. Siddhartha didn't move. Then the Master of Illusions made rain fall so that all the country was flooded. None of the water touched Siddhartha. The blazing rocks Mara threw changed into flowers.

"Kill him!" Mara screamed at his soldiers. They let their arrows fly and they attacked with swords and axes. But Siddhartha's light was his shield. The swords broke against it, and arrows turned to flowers when they touched the ground. The soldiers stopped and stared. Terrified, they threw down their weapons and ran away.

"I have lost!" Mara cried. And he too ran away.

Meanwhile, Siddhartha sat calmly in the shade of the Bodhi tree, aware of all that happened. Nothing disturbed him. Without fear, without hope, he kept his mind quiet and looked inward, waiting for enlightenment.

Gradually, in the stillness of his meditation, understanding dawned. He began to see the way beyond suffering. If a person could learn to avoid all selfish desires, all attachment to the things of this world, he or she might not have to live and die and be reborn in an endless cycle.

That person would join with the spirit world, which connects everything in the universe, and be at peace.

Siddhartha's heart and mind told him that the path to follow is the Middle Way—living not for the extremes of pleasure or self-denial, but for tranquility. Here lay the true meaning of life, and when Siddhartha felt this, he became the Awakened One —the Buddha.

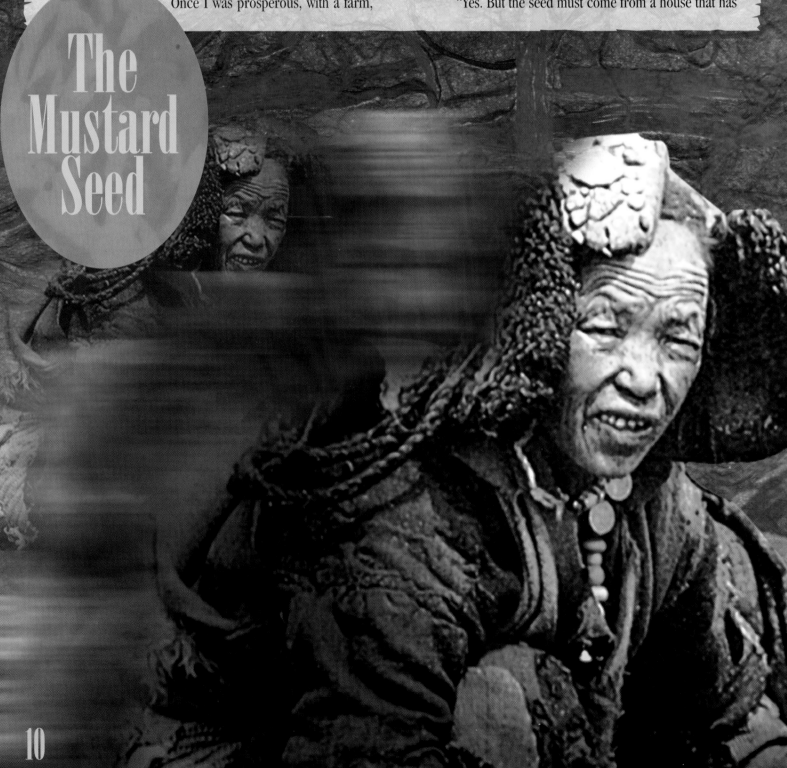

The Mustard Seed

The Buddha was walking on a dusty country road one day when he stopped at the edge of a river to splash cooling water on his face. When he finished washing, he looked up and saw an old woman kneeling beside him. Her clothes were ragged and her face was worn. Her arms were covered with sores.

"Oh, Master," she wailed. "I suffer so. Please help me."

"What troubles you?" the Buddha asked, looking at her with compassion in his eyes.

"Look at me! See my sad lot!" She touched her rags, and she pointed with skinny fingers to her blistered arms. "I am poor, my clothes are torn, I am ill. Once I was prosperous, with a farm, and now I am old and have only a bowl of rice to eat. Won't you heal me and bring back my riches?"

"You have described life as it is," the Buddha answered. "We are all born to suffering."

The old woman shook her head, weeping. "No, no, I won't listen. I was not born to suffer."

The Buddha saw that she could not understand. "Very well, I will help you," he said. "You must do as I say."

"Anything, anything!" she gasped.

"Bring me a mustard seed."

She stared in astonishment. "Only a mustard seed?"

"Yes. But the seed must come from a house that has

never known sorrow, trouble, or suffering. I will take the seed and use it to banish all your misery."

"Thank you, Master, thank you!"

The old woman hobbled away, her bare feet shuffling in the dust. She was on her way to find a house without sorrow. The Buddha continued down the road.

Weeks later, he returned along the same road and came to the same place by the river, and there he saw the old woman again. She was scrubbing clothes in the river water and spreading them on rocks to dry in the sun, and while she washed, she sang a tune.

"Greetings," the Buddha said. "Have you found the mustard seed?"

"No, Blessed One. Every house I visited had far more troubles than I have."

"And are you still seeking?"

"I'll do that later. I have met so many people who are less fortunate than I, I have to stop and help them. Right now I'm washing clothes for a poor family with sick children." Gently she placed a wet piece of cloth on a rock.

The Buddha smiled. He said, "You no longer need the mustard seed. Helping others is a great virtue. You are on the road to becoming a Buddha yourself."

The Enchanted Lake

Once there was a boy named Tashi who lived at the foot of a high mountain in Tibet. All his life Tashi had heard about an enchanted lake on the top of the mountain—a lake that was filled with treasure. Oh, how he wanted to climb the mountain and find that wonderful lake! He dreamed of it night and day and thought about all the things he could buy with the money he would pull from the water.

"Tashi, it's dangerous there," his parents warned him. "Others have tried before you. The spirit who guards the lake does not look kindly upon intruders."

But Tashi was determined. Early one morning, wearing a warm coat and carrying an empty sack, he began to climb the mountain. Higher and higher he went, up to the icy slopes where the wind howled without ceasing, and on to the very top. The air was misty and cold, and the only sound was the whistling wind. Pulling his coat tighter around him, Tashi scrambled over a pile of rocks, and there it was—the enchanted lake.

Every lake Tashi had ever seen was a deep blue, but this one shimmered like gold. "Treasure is there, and it's all mine!" he told himself, and he hurried to the shore.

Suddenly, as he stared greedily at the golden lake, a figure rose from the water. It was a gigantic woman, wearing a gold necklace and a cloak of coarse brown wool. Water streamed from her long, wild hair. Her face was ferocious.

Remembering the warnings, Tashi trembled before the spirit of the lake. But the glittering water made him bold. He said, "I have come for treasure. What do you have for me?"

"More for those who need and don't ask than for those who demand," the spirit answered.

"I want my share!"

"Then take it and go." And the figure vanished.

Tashi reached into the cold, sparkling water. He felt something, grabbed for it, and brought up three gold coins. "I've got it!" he exclaimed. He looked at the coins and back at the water. "Where there is some, there must be more," he muttered. "If I get help, we can take twice as much." And he dropped his sack and tossed the coins back into the lake. He hurried down the mountain, stumbling over rocks and roots, and back home.

When he got there, he told his father about his adventure. "The spirit is no danger, and the lake is full of money. We can take big bags and fill them up. We'll be rich."

Tashi's father agreed that this was a grand opportunity. And so, carrying two large bags, they climbed the mountain. Over the icy slopes and up to the top they went, and they found the shimmering lake just as Tashi had first seen it. When they reached the shore, the spirit woman rose again, huge and

majestic, dripping glittering drops of water.

"Now what do you want?" she demanded. "I gave you three golden coins. Wasn't that enough?"

Tashi said, "My father said he had to see the lake for himself. Give him a share too, and we won't bother you again."

A cloud swirled around the figure, and when it cleared, she was gone.

The boy and his father immediately reached into the water and grabbed at the bottom. Each brought up three gold coins.

"Ahhh," Tashi's father sighed.

"Didn't I tell you? The lake is full of money. Let's get the rest of the family, and a yak to carry the load, and take out all we can. We'll never have to plow the fields again."

They tossed their bags and few coins into the lake and descended the mountain. By the time they reached home and gathered their excited relatives, night had fallen. It was too dark to return.

"The lake will be there tomorrow," Tashi said. "Let's celebrate our good fortune tonight and go back in the morning."

This seemed a good idea, so the family invited the entire village in to feast on the food in the storeroom and the barley beer that was laid aside for the winter. "We can soon buy more," Tashi said. The party lasted far into the night.

The next day, Tashi led his parents and brothers and sisters up the mountain. With them plodded a yak, carrying huge, empty bags. The closer they got to the top, and the more Tashi bragged about his find, the more excited they all became. Everyone agreed that it would be grand to fill the big packs with treasure and be the richest family in the village.

"This is the place," Tashi announced at last, "just beyond those rocks." They struggled over the rocks, and there was the lake. But this was not the lake that Tashi had described. There was no golden water, no guardian spirit. There were only fog and mist and silence.

Tashi rushed to the shore. "I'm here!" he called. "I've come for more gold coins." He plunged his hand into the icy water and grabbed at the bottom. Nothing. He fished again and the others tried, but not a coin did they find. All day they waded in the mountain lake, searching, bringing up nothing but mud and pebbles.

There was no boasting about riches on the long walk home. By the time they got to the cold, empty house, it was nightfall, and they were exhausted and hungry. For dinner they had a cup of broth, all that was left of their food.

High on the mountain top, the lake gleamed under a round, golden moon.

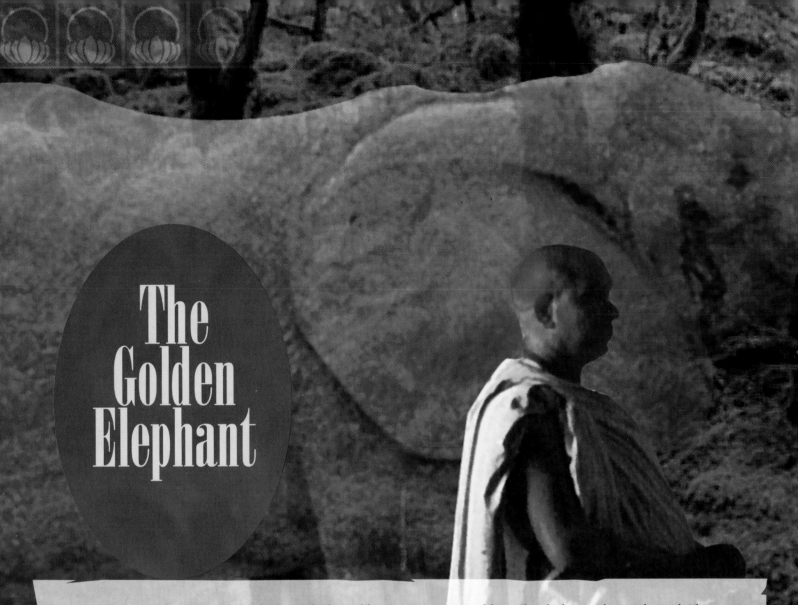

The Golden Elephant

In a kingdom in India, there lived a boy who had a golden elephant. The baby elephant had appeared in the family courtyard the moment the boy, whose name was Gopala, was born.

Gopala and his elephant grew up together like brothers. Wherever Gopala went, the elephant followed, and crowds would gather to see them. Everything about this amazing pet was gold, even his urine and droppings!

One day a messenger from the king came to Gopala's home. "The king orders you to bring your elephant to the palace," he announced. "All golden elephants belong to the royal household and may not be kept as pets by the common people."

Gopala said to his father, "My elephant is like my twin brother. How can the king take him away?"

"The king is jealous and greedy," his father replied. "We must go to the palace as he commands and hope that justice will prevail."

Gopala stroked the elephant's shining trunk. He was afraid that he might lose his dearest friend, but he whispered, "Don't worry, all will be well."

The elephant knelt so Gopala and his father could climb on his back, and off they rode to the palace. When they arrived, the king dismissed them with a wave of his hand. "Be on your way, and leave the elephant with me," he said. The many rings on his fingers gleamed in the sun, but none shone as brightly as the elephant's golden back. The king smiled, proud that he was now the owner of such a precious animal.

Gopala looked at his father in dismay. Couldn't he do something? But his father just bowed to the king, calmly took Gopala's arm, and walked away from the palace.

"The king has stolen my elephant!" Gopala complained as they headed home. "This is wrong and unfair."

"Be patient, my son," his father said.

As they approached the edge of the forest, Gopala heard a familiar sound. He looked up in surprise, and there stood the golden elephant, waiting for him.

His father smiled and said, "Last night I dreamed that your pet would come back to us. I knew he would be here."

They returned home happily and never heard from the king again. But Gopala felt sad because he lived in a land where a king would steal from his subjects. As he grew older, Gopala saw more injustices, and he noticed how people were always wanting things they didn't have. They were jealous, like the king, and never happy.

Time passed, and Gopala began to turn away from the world of daily concerns and material things. He spent more time

thinking and meditating. He gave away almost all his possessions, he helped the poor, and finally he decided to renounce ordinary life. He would go to the Buddha and ask to be accepted as a monk.

It wasn't long before Gopala, seated on his elephant, was on his way to the Buddha. When they arrived, the elephant knelt so Gopala could dismount and approach with reverence, on foot.

The Buddha welcomed him. Compassion and love shone in his eyes as he said, "Come now, into a life of purity."

As soon as those words were spoken, Gopala was transformed into a monk. His long black hair was gone, he was wearing a monk's yellow robe, and in his hands was a bowl for begging. Like every Buddhist monk, he would own nothing and beg for rice every day. He even had a new name: Kanakavatsa.

Everything about Kanakavatsa's old life was left behind, except one thing—the golden elephant. Kanakavatsa had learned to stop thinking about and longing for possessions. He felt free of such concerns, even as the elephant remained by his side.

Kanakavatsa was a good monk. But he attracted a lot of attention, because the people who gathered to hear him teach the Way of the Buddha were fascinated by the amazing elephant.

Some of them could talk of nothing else, and they even quarreled over the animal's golden dung. When the Buddha heard of this, he sent for Kanakavatsa. "Your elephant is creating a disturbance," he said. "You are not to blame, but your pet must go."

Kanakavatsa said, "I understand. I'm ready to release my last worldly connection. But he has been my faithful friend all my life. I want him to gain wisdom and feel the same contentment I have found."

"We are all brothers," the Buddha said. "We all long for a peaceful spirit. Your golden elephant came to you because of your own good actions in past lives—your karma. To free him from his own bondage, tell him you have fulfilled your purpose. He must do the same."

Kanakavatsa went to the elephant, who was quietly chewing leaves at the edge of the forest. "Dear friend," he said, stroking the animal's side, "thank you for your companionship and brotherhood. We no longer need each other. I am free and contented, and I want this for you, too. Go in peace."

Three times Kanakavatsa said this, and as he said, "Go in peace" for the third time, the elephant dissolved before his eyes. For an instant, a spot of shimmering gold hung in the air, and then all was gone and there was silence among the trees.

DO UNTO OTHERS
AS YOU WOULD
HAVE THEM DO
UNTO YOU

Christia

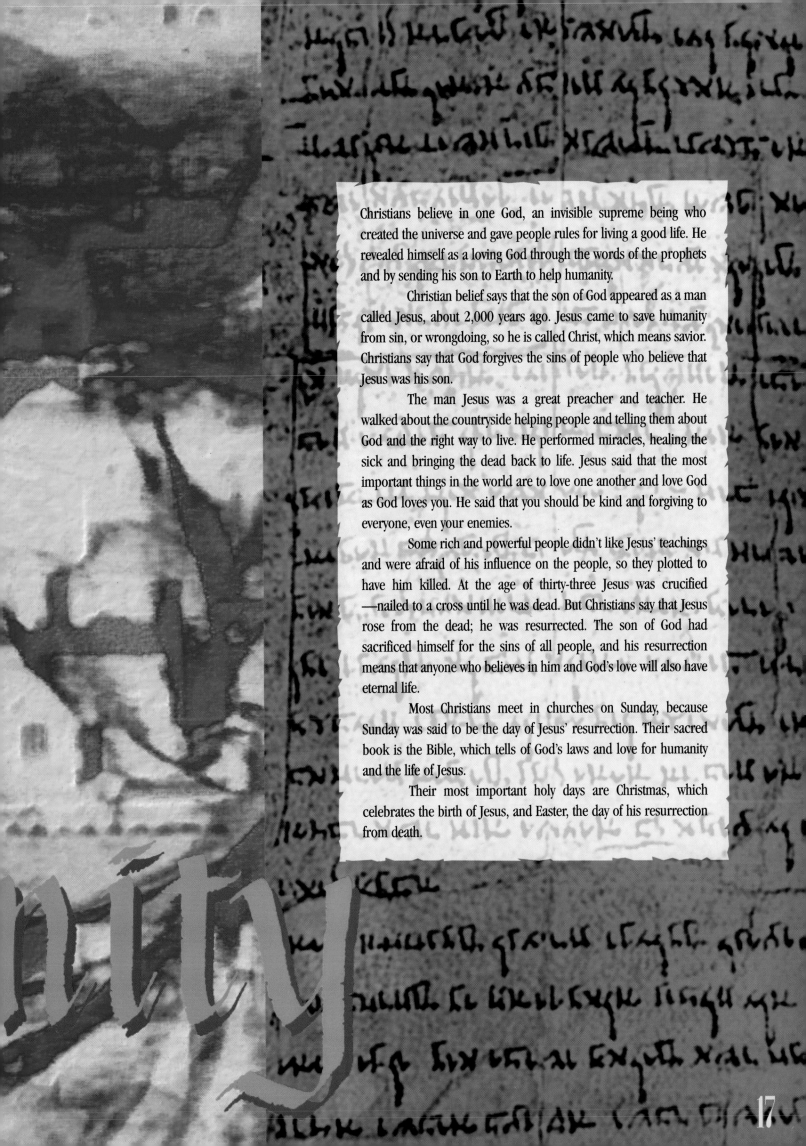

Christians believe in one God, an invisible supreme being who created the universe and gave people rules for living a good life. He revealed himself as a loving God through the words of the prophets and by sending his son to Earth to help humanity.

Christian belief says that the son of God appeared as a man called Jesus, about 2,000 years ago. Jesus came to save humanity from sin, or wrongdoing, so he is called Christ, which means savior. Christians say that God forgives the sins of people who believe that Jesus was his son.

The man Jesus was a great preacher and teacher. He walked about the countryside helping people and telling them about God and the right way to live. He performed miracles, healing the sick and bringing the dead back to life. Jesus said that the most important things in the world are to love one another and love God as God loves you. He said that you should be kind and forgiving to everyone, even your enemies.

Some rich and powerful people didn't like Jesus' teachings and were afraid of his influence on the people, so they plotted to have him killed. At the age of thirty-three Jesus was crucified —nailed to a cross until he was dead. But Christians say that Jesus rose from the dead; he was resurrected. The son of God had sacrificed himself for the sins of all people, and his resurrection means that anyone who believes in him and God's love will also have eternal life.

Most Christians meet in churches on Sunday, because Sunday was said to be the day of Jesus' resurrection. Their sacred book is the Bible, which tells of God's laws and love for humanity and the life of Jesus.

Their most important holy days are Christmas, which celebrates the birth of Jesus, and Easter, the day of his resurrection from death.

The Birth of Jesus

For many years, prophets had foretold the birth of the son of God. He would come to Earth as a man to save people from their sins and promise eternal life.

In the city of Nazareth, in Judaea, an angel appeared one day to a young woman named Mary. Mary was afraid. The angel said to her, "Mary, you are blessed. Do not fear, you have found favor with God. You shall bear a son called Jesus, and he shall be the son of the highest. Of his kingdom there shall be no end."

Mary said, "How can this be? I am not yet married to Joseph, and no man could be the father."

The angel said, "God will make it happen. With God nothing is impossible."

Mary rejoiced. Mary and Joseph were married. Months went by, and the emperor of the land announced that every man must go to the city of his birth to pay taxes.

So Joseph and Mary traveled to Bethlehem, the city where Joseph was born.

When they got there, exhausted after their long journey, they saw a crowded city. They tried to get a room at the inn, and they were told that every corner was taken. But Mary and Joseph found a place to stay. They slept in a shed for animals, and there Jesus was born. They wrapped the baby tenderly in swaddling clothes and laid him in a manger.

Out in the fields, under the bright stars, shepherds were watching their sheep. Suddenly a glorious angel appeared, and the shepherds were filled with fear. The angel said, "Fear not. I bring you good tidings of great joy. Unto you is born this day a Savior, Christ the Lord. You shall find him in a manger." Other angels appeared, all of them praising God.

When the angels were gone, the shepherds hurried

to Bethlehem and found the baby and knelt reverently before him.

Wise men far to the East saw a brilliant star in the night sky. They knew this must be the star that the prophets had said would shine when the new King of the Jews was born, and so they followed it to the city of Jerusalem. In Jerusalem, they asked, "Where is he that is born King of the Jews? We have come to worship him."

King Herod heard of these happenings, and he called in his chief priests and demanded to know where this child was. They told him, "The prophets say, in Bethlehem of Judaea."

Herod told the wise men, "Go search for the child, and when you have found him, let me know so I can come and worship him also." But Herod was not interested in worship. He had other plans for this child who might become a king and threaten his power.

The wise men followed the star, found the child, and rejoiced. They fell on their knees and gave him gifts: gold, frankincense, and myrrh. But God warned them in a dream not to go back to King Herod, so they went to their own country another way. When the wise men did not return, Herod was furious. He told his soldiers, "Go to Bethlehem and all the towns around it, and kill every child under two years of age."

An angel appeared to Joseph in a dream. "Arise," he said. "Take the child and his mother and flee into Egypt, and stay there until I bring word. Herod will try to destroy the child."

Joseph and Mary and Jesus escaped by night to Egypt, as the angel told them, and they did not return to their home in Nazareth until the angel appeared and said that all was safe again.

The Good Samaritan

One day a lawyer asked Jesus, "Master, what must I do to live for eternity?"

Jesus said, "What is written in the law?"

The lawyer answered, "You shall love the Lord your God with all your heart, and with all your soul, and with all your strength, and with all your mind, and your neighbor as yourself."

Jesus said, "You have answered right: do this, and you shall live."

"But Master," the lawyer said, "who is my neighbor?" Jesus answered with this story:

A man was walking on a lonely stretch of road between Jerusalem and Jericho, when a gang of thieves jumped out from the side of the road and demanded his money. The man resisted; he needed that money to buy goods for his family. One of the thieves scooped up a rock and hit the man on the head. Wounded, the man groaned and fell.

The thieves glanced around. No one was in sight. "Take everything!" one said. They stripped off his clothing, stole his money, and hit him again before they ran away, leaving the man half-dead.

After a time, a priest came walking down the road. He saw the man lying on the dusty ground, and he hurried on by.

Soon another man, a Levite, appeared. He, too, saw the wounded man lying in the hot sun, naked and bleeding,

and he scurried away.

A long time passed. Flies buzzed over the man, who would soon die of his injuries. But someone else was traveling that road. He was a Samaritan, riding his donkey. Now the people of Samaria were not friendly with the people of the wounded man's country. They mistrusted and even hated each other.

This Samaritan, though, did not hesitate when he saw the man on the road. He did not stop to think whether the man was a friend or not. He saw that this was someone who desperately needed help, and he felt compassion.

The Samaritan took healing oil and wine from his bag and cleaned the man's wounds and covered him with a robe. He gave him a drink of water and helped the man onto the donkey. Slowly they walked to the next town, where the Samaritan found an inn and made the man comfortable. Before he left the next day, he gave money to the innkeeper to pay for the room and to take care of the man until he had recovered.

When Jesus finished telling this story, he asked, "Which of these three men was neighbor to the man who fell among thieves?"

The lawyer who had asked, "Who is my neighbor?" said, "The one who showed mercy."

Jesus said, "Go and do the same."

21

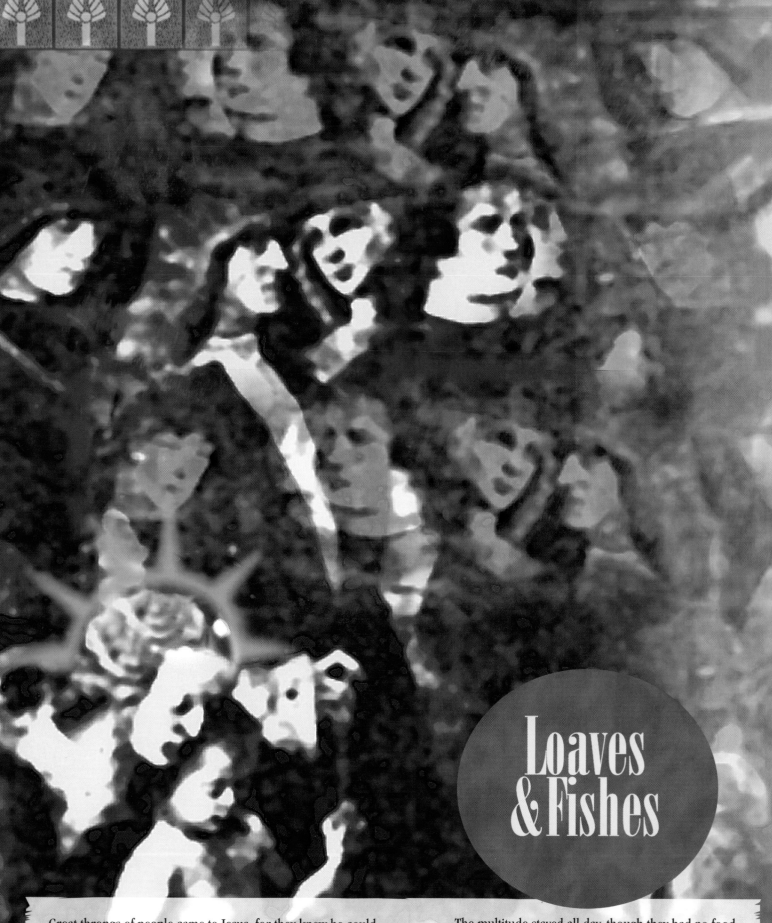

Loaves & Fishes

Great throngs of people came to Jesus, for they knew he could cause the dumb to speak, the maimed to be whole, the lame to walk, and the blind to see. They walked from the cities far into the countryside to see him and listen to his words.

One day a huge crowd gathered, thousands of people, all eager to be near him. When Jesus touched or spoke to a sick person, that person was healed.

The multitude stayed all day, though they had no food and they could find little shade from the hot sun. When it was evening, Jesus' disciples said, "It's getting late. Send these people home to their cities and villages so they can buy food for themselves."

"They need not depart; give them food," Jesus answered. The disciples were surprised. Surely Jesus didn't

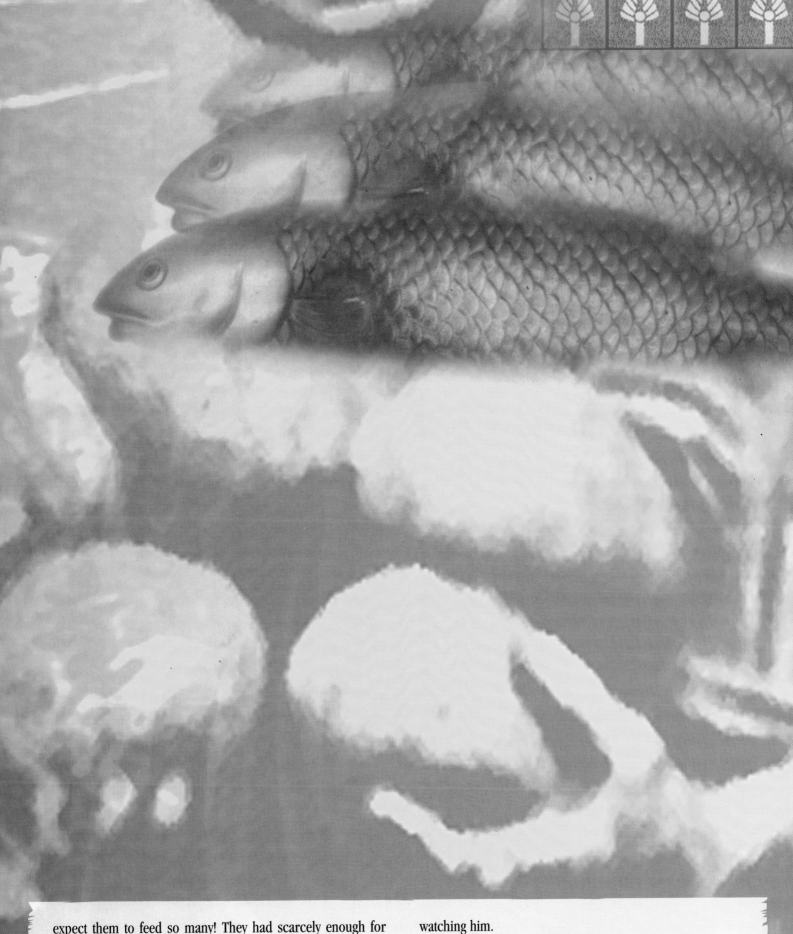

expect them to feed so many! They had scarcely enough for themselves. They said, "We have only five loaves of bread and two fishes."

He said, "Bring them to me."

He told the people to sit on the ground. Holding the loaves and fishes in his hands, he raised his arms and looked up to heaven and blessed the food. The hungry crowd hushed, watching him.

Jesus gave the bread and fish to his disciples and said, "Now share this food." The disciples put the blessed food in baskets and walked among the people. Many hands reached into the baskets and took out bread and fish. Yet the baskets never emptied. Everyone ate and was filled.

Five thousand people were fed that day.

Mary, Martha, & Lazarus

Jesus had been going from town to town teaching and preaching all day. When he and his disciples reached the village of Bethany, they knew they would be welcome in the home of friends. There they would rest and refresh themselves. The friends were two sisters, Mary and Martha, and their brother, Lazarus.

Martha saw them coming. "I'm not through sweeping the floor, and Jesus and his followers are almost here!" she said. "I hope we have enough food for everyone."

"Don't worry, Jesus won't notice or think the worse of us," Mary said.

Martha quickly finished sweeping, wiped her hands, and hurried to the door. "Welcome, all of you," she said. "Please come in and rest yourselves. Let me bring you cool water and wine. We have bread and olives and cakes for you. Please sit down, everything will be ready in a moment."

While she was talking, the guests entered the small home and found cushions and benches to sit upon. Martha

bustled off to the kitchen.

When she came back carrying trays of food, she saw her sister seated on the floor beside Jesus, listening to him talk. Martha set the food on the table and turned to Jesus. She said, "Lord, don't you care that my sister has left me to serve alone? Tell her to come help me."

Jesus turned to her. His voice was gentle. "Martha, Martha, you are so careful, and you worry about so many things. Only one thing is really important, and Mary has chosen it. I would not take it from her."

Martha knew what Jesus was telling her. The most important thing was learning about God's message of love and everlasting life.

After that visit Martha and Mary didn't see Jesus again until they were weeping in sorrow, for their brother, Lazarus, had died. When Martha saw Jesus walking along the road toward her village, she ran to him and said, "Lord, if you had been here, my

brother would not have died."

Jesus looked into her tear-swollen eyes. "Do you believe that whoever believes in me shall never die?"

"Yes, Lord, I believe you are the son of God come into the world."

Mary came with their friends and family, all of them mourning the death of Lazarus. Jesus wept, too. He asked, "Where have you laid him?" And they said, "Come and see."

They went to the tomb, carved into a rock wall. "Roll the stone away," Jesus said.

Martha shook her head. "Lord, it's too late. He has been dead for four days."

Jesus said, "Martha, didn't I say that if you believe you will see the glory of God?"

Two strong men rolled the stone away. Jesus looked up to the heavens and said, "Father, thank you for hearing me. I do this only so the people will believe you have sent me."

Silence fell over the group. Everyone sensed that something extraordinary was about to happen. They were startled when Jesus called out in a loud voice, "Lazarus, come forth."

The people watching scarcely breathed. A tense moment went by. From the depths of the dark tomb, a figure appeared, walking, bound with linens that covered even the face.

"Lazarus!" Mary murmured.

"Free him from the grave cloths, and let him go," Jesus said.

Martha ran to Lazarus and began to pull at the cloths. "My brother, my dear brother!" she exclaimed. When he stepped into the daylight, smiling, he was as whole and healthy as if nothing had happened.

Mary, Martha, and Lazarus fell to their knees and kissed the dust-covered hem of Jesus' robe. Jesus said nothing. He touched them with compassion and went on his way, while the people watched in awe and wonder.

The Resurrection

Jesus was dead. Those who loved him had watched him die in pain, crucified on a cross, and when he was dead, they took him down and wrapped his body in clean linen cloths. They laid the body in a tomb carved in rock, covered the opening of the tomb with a huge stone, and went sadly away.

All was quiet. Three days went by.

On the morning of the first day of the week, just at dawn, three women—Mary Magdalene, Salome, and Mary the mother of James—came to the tomb carrying spices to anoint the body. They weren't sure how they would get into the tomb; they knew it was blocked by the heavy stone.

To their surprise, the stone had been rolled away from the entrance. "Who has done this?" they wondered.

The women went slowly into the tomb, and there they saw, seated on a bench in the rock, a young man wearing a long white garment. His face glowed with light, and radiance surrounded him. Terrified, the two Marys and Salome dropped their spice jars and turned to run.

The man said, "Do not be afraid. I know you seek Jesus, who was crucified. He is not here, for he is risen. See, here is the place where his body was laid."

The women looked. It was true, Jesus' body was gone. Only the white burial cloth was left. "Go quickly now," the man continued. "Tell his disciples that Jesus is risen from the dead."

In fear and joy they left the tomb. "Can it be true? Is Jesus alive?" they asked each other. "Was that radiant man an angel sent by God?"

As they hurried along the road to find the disciples and tell them the news, someone spoke to them. They knew that voice very well. "It's Jesus!" And there he was, standing before them. They fell to their knees.

"Do not be afraid," Jesus said. "Go tell my friends that I am alive and you have seen me."

The women found the disciples together, weeping and mourning the loss of their beloved master.

"Weep no longer," Mary Magdalene said. "Jesus is alive! We have seen him."

The disciples saw her happiness, and their hearts leaped with hope. But the hope faded, and they shook their heads. "Foolish woman," one said. "He has been dead for three days. The best man who ever lived is gone forever."

Another sighed and said, "Her grief has made her mad. Leave her alone."

With heavy hearts they sat down to eat. Suddenly the room was filled with a dazzling light. They closed their eyes against the brightness, and when they opened them again, they saw Jesus standing beside the table.

"Oh my brothers," Jesus said, "you have so little faith. Why do you not believe the words of those who have seen me?" He held out his hands. "Look at my hands. See my feet. There are the marks of the nails from the cross. Now will you believe?"

"Master, we believe," they cried.

Jesus smiled at his friends. "Peace be unto you," he said. "I am with you always, even unto the end of the world."

They talked together, happy again. A few days later, they went into the countryside, where Jesus taught them to open their understanding of his message of love. And as he blessed them, he raised his arms and was carried up to heaven to be with God.

Now, although Jesus was gone, the disciples no longer mourned. With joy they worshipped him and went to the temple in Jerusalem to praise God and spread the word of the resurrection.

TREAT OTHERS AS YOU WOULD YOURSELF BE TREATED

Hindu

Hinduism began in India thousands of years ago and is still the main religion of India and Nepal.

Hindus believe that every person's spirit is a part of the great spirit of the universe they call Brahman. This great spirit is eternal and everywhere, with no beginning and no end, and it has no form that can be pictured. But the many gods and goddesses worshipped by Hindus each represent one aspect of Brahman. The three most significant gods are Brahma, the Creator; Vishnu, the Protector; and Shiva, the Destroyer.

Hinduism teaches nonviolence, truthfulness, respect for parents and the elderly, simple living, and helping the needy.

One of Hinduism's most important beliefs is reincarnation, which means that after your body dies, your soul is reborn in another form. If you have lived a moral life, you will be reincarnated on a higher level; if not, you may come back as an animal or insect or a person of lower status. If you gain spiritual knowledge and try to do good, your spirit may reach a oneness with Brahman, and you will have perfect happiness and not have to come back to earthly life again.

Hindus have all kinds of rich and colorful ceremonies, festivals, and rituals. Most people keep a small shrine at home, and in temples large and small, they stop to pray and leave a flower on their way to work.

The Birth of Krishna

There was once a good and rich man named Vasudeva, who lived in the city of Mathura, in India. He was married to a woman named Devaki. On the happy day of their wedding, a priest who could foresee the future told them that Devaki's eighth son would grow up to kill a cruel tyrant, the wicked King Kamsa. The boy would become the ruler of Mathura, the priest said, taking the place of the king.

Time went by, and the prediction was forgotten by almost everyone—everyone but King Kamsa, who was angry that a priest had said his throne and his life might be taken from him.

Devaki and Vasudeva had seven sons. When it came time for their eighth child to be born, King Kamsa heard about it, and he flew into a rage. "Throw Vasudeva and Devaki in prison," he ordered. "I want them locked up, behind bars. Their eighth child will never see the light of day."

It was a cold, rainy winter, the coldest it had ever been in Mathura, when the soldiers took Vasudeva and Devaki to jail. They were locked in dirty rooms, and they slept on straw. Their eighth son was born in the straw, with candles the only light. Strangely, his skin was pure blue, as blue as the sky. His parents named him Krishna.

That night, Vasudeva knew they must escape. King Kamsa would never let the boy leave the prison alive. But how could they get past the guards and through the bars and over the high walls?

In the darkness, when all was quiet, Vasudeva heard a voice. "Take your baby away, into the land of Braj. There he will be safe. Go now, go quickly!"

In wonderment, Vasudeva wrapped the little blue baby in a shawl and went to the locked prison door. Silently, it slid open. He saw guards in the corridor; they were all sound asleep, with keys dangling from their hands. He walked past them to the heavy gates, and the gates swung open.

Vasudeva went into the city's dark, deserted streets and continued on to the countryside. He walked and walked, carrying the sleeping child. When he came to the edge of the Jamuna River, he saw that the water was high and running fast. "How can I

cross?" Vasudeva wondered in despair. "There is no ferry, and the river is too swift to wade or swim."

At that moment, the baby Krishna wakened and stuck his foot out from the shawl. Instantly the roaring ceased, and the waves grew still, and the water sank away into the sand. Clutching the baby, Vasudeva hurried across the river bottom to the other side. He continued walking, and at last he reached the home of a cowherd in a village in Braj.

That same night, a baby girl had been born to the cowherd, who was a kindly man named Nanda, and his wife, Jasodha. Vasudeva switched the babies. Tenderly, he put little Krishna in the wooden cradle and carried the other child away, back to the Mathura prison. He hoped that when King Kamsa saw that the child was a girl, he would believe that he was safe from the priest's prophecy.

In the morning, Kamsa's servants came for Vasudeva and Devaki and brought them and the baby to the king. He sat proudly on his throne in the courtyard, where sweet-smelling flowers bloomed.

"So this is your eighth child," Kamsa said, with an ugly frown. "Yes, King Kamsa, and she is a girl, no threat to you."

Suddenly the king stood and marched across the courtyard, his red robes flowing and jewels flashing. He reached out and snatched the baby from Devaki's arms and lifted her, ready to throw her to the ground and kill her. Vasudeva and Devaki cried out, "No!"

But as soon as King Kamsa held the child high, she flew from his hands and was transformed into the goddess Devi. In her eight strong arms she held a trident, a sword, a pot full of honey, and a lotus blossom. Pearls hung around her neck, her robes were blue and gold, and a crown rested on her shining hair. Her bracelets and anklets were peacock feathers. Blue flames burned around her, and as she rose into the sky, in a voice like thunder she said, "Your doom is sealed, King Kamsa. Krishna is safe. The little blue child is not an ordinary child, he is the high god Vishnu, come to earth to help all people." And off Devi flew to dance and sing with the other gods and goddesses.

Shiva, Parvati, & The Elephant God Ganesh

Long, long ago, the goddess Parvati, daughter of the mountain, went to her husband Shiva and said, "Oh, Shiva, I yearn for a child. Unite with me today, and let us have a son. Then you will have descendants to perform rituals for you."

The four-armed god Shiva, destroyer of evil and lord of the dance, said, "Parvati, I have no need of a son, because I will never die. I will have no use for the rituals done for ancestors. Let us enjoy our pleasures without a child."

Parvati, holding two lotus flowers in her hands, answered, "That is true, great lord, but I still wish to have a child. I will care for him by myself."

Still Shiva refused. But when he heard Parvati's sad sigh, he said, "All right. If you want the face of a son to kiss, I will make one for you." And he pulled a piece of cloth from her red gown and said, "Here is your son."

Parvati said, "You are teasing me, Lord Shiva. This is a piece of my dress, not a child." She formed it into the shape of a baby and held it to her breast. As she did so, to her surprise the cloth began to quiver and come to life. Delighted, Parvati stroked the moving, baby-shaped cloth with the lotus flowers, and the boy began to breathe. "Mama, Mama!" he cried.

Instantly she took him to her breasts and lovingly fed him. The boy gazed at his mother and felt her love.

Parvati handed the child to Shiva. "See my beautiful son, Shiva. Now I am happy."

Shiva smiled. "I gave you a son from cloth to tease you, and he became a true son. This is a miracle." He took the boy and looked at him closely. "But your son was born with an

injury," he said. "He will not live long."

At that moment, the child's head broke from its body and fell to the ground. Parvati, overcome with grief, screamed and wept.

"Parvati, my dear, do not cry. We will bring him to life again," Shiva said. He called his servant Nandin. "Bring us a head, one with no injury, for Parvati's son," he said. "Search the universe until you find it."

After a long time, Nandin returned. "I have found the head, oh Shiva," he said. "It is the head of an elephant! I had to fight for it in a ferocious battle, because it was the head of the king of the elephants of Indra, the war god."

Shiva took the elephant head and placed it on the child's shoulders, and at once the boy came to life again. He shone with a special beauty. Parvati's little son was a short, fat god, with a round belly, a rosy red elephant face, four arms, and three eyes. The other gods came to see him, bringing presents: a writing pen and colored inks, beads, a lotus, a bowl of sweets, a tiger skin. The goddess Earth gave him a rat to ride on.

Brahma the creator said, "Call him Ganesh, meaning Ruler. Anyone who wants to take a journey or start something new should think of Ganesh, and he will remove any obstacles."

As for Indra's elephant, Shiva said, "Throw the elephant's body into the ocean, Indra, and he will arise from the waves alive again."

The goddess Parvati rejoiced and cared well for Ganesh, who became a great and wise god, beloved by the people.

Rama, Sita & The Ten Thousand Monkeys

Once there was a prince named Rama. He was handsome, brave, strong, and good, loved by everyone in the kingdom of Ayodhya. His wife, Princess Sita, was so beautiful, so gentle and kind that everywhere she went, people strewed jasmine and rose petals in her path.

Rama's wise father, Dasaratha the rajah, or king, saw that his son would be a virtuous ruler. "I am getting old and tired," he said. "I shall crown my oldest son, Rama, as the rajah and spend the rest of my days at leisure with my three wives."

The people rejoiced, and a great celebration was planned. But the night before the coronation, when Dasaratha came to see his favorite wife, he found her crying. He said, "My beloved, what is the matter? Tomorrow is a happy event, you should not be weeping."

She cried harder. She was jealous. Why should Prince Rama, the son of another wife, be crowned rajah, and not her son?

"Tell me why you cry," Dasaratha said, stroking her hair. "Whatever you want, I will give to you. Pearls, jewels, cities, anything."

"Do you promise?" she asked. "Anything?"

"Of course, my love," he said with a fond smile.

"I demand that Rama be sent to live in the jungle for fourteen years, and my son crowned in his place."

Dasaratha was stricken with horror, but he had given his word. With great sadness he ordered Rama to leave the palace.

When Princess Sita heard the news, she said, "I'm going with you, Rama. My place is by your side."

Rama shook his head. "No, Sita, my dear, the jungle is dangerous, full of snakes and tigers. I will have to eat wild fruits and sleep among the leaves." But Sita insisted, and so together they went into the deep green wilderness. Lakshman,

another of Rama's brothers, went with them.

Through thick tangles of vines they walked. They drank water from bubbling springs, hunted for their food and slept on the grass and in caves.

Finally, in the land of monkeys, Rama and Sita and Lakshman stopped. They built a pretty home of bamboo. They agreed, "Here we will live the rest of our years in the wilderness."

One day a strange woman came to the door. She wanted Rama for herself and was jealous of Sita. When Rama refused to leave Sita, the woman fled to her brother, the demon Ravan. "Avenge me, Ravan!" she shrieked. "Kill Rama and Lakshman, and you can have the beautiful Princess Sita."

Ravan, ruler of an island kingdom, agreed to do as his sister said. He devised a wicked plan. He turned one of his demons into a golden deer with jeweled antlers and sent it to the river bank where Sita often walked. When the princess saw the enchanted deer, she yearned to have it. She returned to the cottage and said, "I am lonely, Rama, and the deer would be good company." So Rama went to capture the deer, and Lakshman stayed behind to protect Sita.

After a while a strange noise echoed through the jungle. Sita was frightened. She cried, "It sounds like Rama! He's in trouble! You must go to help him."

Lakshman grabbed his bow and arrow, but before he left, he drew a line around the cottage and said, "Sita, you are safe in this circle. Do not cross it, and no harm will come to you."

Sita agreed. "Now go, hurry to Rama," she urged. She sat by the door of the cottage to wait, her hair shining black against the red silk of her sari.

Soon a holy man in a ragged robe came near and asked for water. "I'm too tired to come any closer," he said. "Bring it here to me."

Sita filled a cup of water and took it to the old man, who was resting under a tree. She crossed the line of safety. As soon as she reached him, the man threw off his disguise and shouted, "I am Ravan!"

Sita screamed and ran, but Ravan caught her and carried her off in a golden chariot drawn by winged donkeys. High into the air they went, over the trees and mountains to his faraway kingdom.

When Rama and Lakshman returned, they saw that they had been tricked. "The princess has been stolen away! How can we find her?" Lakshman asked anxiously.

"This is the land of the monkeys," his brother answered. "We'll ask them to help."

Fearful for Sita's safety, they hurried to Sugriva, the king of the monkeys. "Please, help us to find Sita and rescue her," they implored.

The monkey king knew of the goodness and power of Rama and Sita. He called his ten thousand monkeys. "Find Sita!" he ordered. "Swing from the vines, climb the high peaks, go as far as the ocean. We must not fail the noble Rama."

It was Hanuman, the monkey king's messenger, who found the captured princess on Ravan's green island. She wore an old cloak, but on it he saw a royal jewel and knew who she was. Hanuman dropped softly from the tree where he was hiding. He placed Rama's ruby ring in her hand.

Overjoyed, the princess gave the monkey a jewel that she had worn in her hair since her wedding day. "Take this to Rama," she whispered. "I am faithful to him and I am waiting. Now run!"

Hanuman jumped into the tree, but he had waited too long. A soldier rushed in, grabbed him, and took him to Ravan. Ravan said, "Tie a rag soaked in oil to this monkey's tail and set it on fire. That will teach him a lesson."

The soldiers obeyed, and soon burning flames

surrounded Hanuman. Trying madly to get away, he leaped around the palace, spreading fire as he went. But Sita's prayers protected him, and the fire subsided. Unharmed, he raced back to Rama and told him where to find his wife.

Down to Ravan's kingdom went Rama, Lakshman, the monkey king, and the ten thousand monkeys. The gates of the city opened and a bloody battle began. Hundreds of arrows flew through the air. The monkeys tossed boulders and trees. Khumba the giant heard the noise and stormed in from his mountain home to help his brother, Ravan. With a push he sent the monkeys reeling. "Where is the famous Rama?" he roared. "He is the only warrior worthy to fight the great Khumba."

As Khumba marched toward the tall prince, Rama shot a flaming arrow from his magic bow. It burned off the giant's hair. Khumba came closer. Rama shot another arrow of fire, and this one pierced Khumba's armor and killed him. Rama threw the body into the sea, where it made a

huge tidal wave.

Seeing all this, Ravan was afraid. He hurried to escape in his golden chariot. The sky darkened and red lightning flashed. The earth shook in anger at so much destruction.

The god Indra watched. "Send my chariot to help Rama," he said. "These warriors must finish the fight." Indra's chariot, drawn by swans, rolled to Rama, and the prince stepped into it and rode like the wind to catch Ravan. Faster and faster the swans flew, until they were close to Ravan's gleaming gold chariot. Rama drew his bow and shot an arrow. It hit its mark, and the demon was killed.

Immediately, music filled the air and flowers rained from the skies, while the monkeys danced in glee. There was joy throughout the land, for Prince Rama and Princess Sita were united again. The fourteen years of exile were over. They returned to their kingdom, and all the monkeys came with them for a long celebration.

The Birth Of The Ganges

Many years ago, in India, a king and queen had sixty thousand sons. The young princes lived happily together in the great palace, and when they were grown, the king, Sagara, decided to hold a celebration of thanks to the gods for sending him so many fine children.

King Sagara issued an order. "Bring out my best horse for this festival," he said. "We must honor the gods for our good fortune."

The horseman found the biggest, handsomest, strongest horse in the stable and led him, tossing his head and prancing, toward the field where King Sagara waited. But before he got there, a demon suddenly appeared and stole the horse away.

Sagara was furious. "The horse must be found and the thief slain!" he said. "If the celebration is not done correctly, the gods will send us bad luck." He called upon his sixty thousand sons and he commanded, "Search the world over, every inch, above the ground or under it. But find that horse and bring him back."

The princes set out. They ranged far and wide, over the mountains and into the valleys, but they could not find the horse or the demon thief. And so, with their mighty hands they began to dig. Trees toppled and rocks flew. The serpents and demons under the earth screeched and roared as the sixty thousand brothers destroyed them. The earth cried out in pain as the princes dug deep into her side.

The gods were alarmed, and they went to the creator god Brahma. "These princes are creating havoc on every creature," they said. "What is to be done?"

Brahma answered, "Vishnu protects the earth. By his wrath, the sons of Sagara will be slain. Do not worry, all of this is fated to happen."

Still the sixty thousand sons plunged into the ground, and the places where they dug became Ocean. While they burrowed, they saw the four elephants who hold up the world. They bowed to each one, and as they passed the fourth elephant, white as the mountain snows, they saw the horse, browsing and grazing. With him was the god Vishnu in the shape of a man.

The brothers rushed at the god and attacked him with trees and boulders. They yelled, "Thief, thief! Now we have you."

From Vishnu's mouth came a mighty roar like thunder, and a crimson flame flashed forth and burned the princes to a pile of ashes.

Now King Sagara knew nothing of this. He called his grandson, Suman, to him. "My sons have not returned with the horse," he said. "Go in search of them."

Suman, too, set out. He searched the world over and went down into the dug-out places. When he came to the four

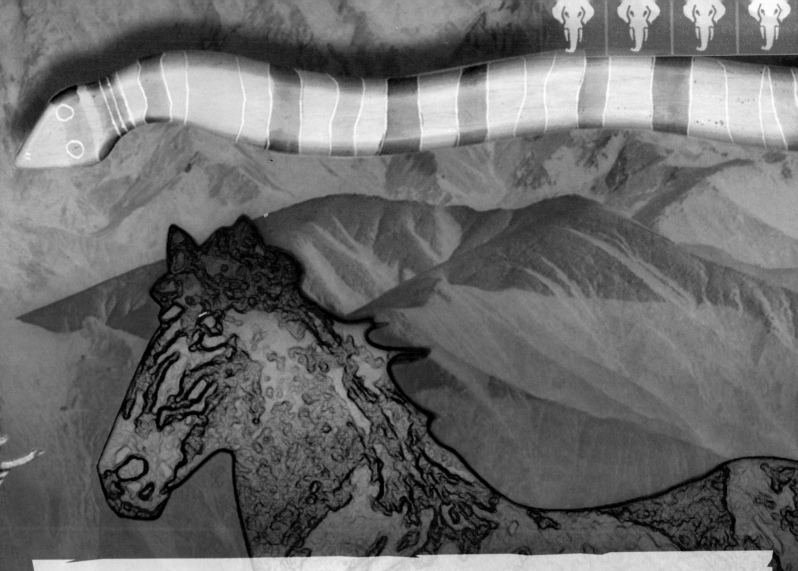

elephants, he bowed to them, and as he passed the fourth elephant he saw the wandering horse and the heap of ashes. He knew what had happened. With a heavy heart Suman wailed his grief. "I cannot even give them the proper funeral rites," he lamented, "because there is no fresh water."

A divine bird, Garuda, was flying through the air above Suman. "Do not grieve, Suman," Garuda called. He flew down to earth and said, "This destruction comes from the gods for the good of all. If you want water to purify the ashes of the sixty thousand brothers, let Ganga come to earth from her sky home. She is the sacred water you need."

Suman took the horse back to King Sagara and told him all that had happened. The king mourned for his sons and longed to give them a funeral ceremony. Without it, their spirits could not be released to heaven. Yet try as he might, he couldn't think of a way to bring Ganga's sacred waters to earth to purify the ashes.

In time Sagara died and another king took his throne, and after him another, and after him another. All of the kings pondered how to bring down Ganga so Sagara's sons could attain their places in heaven.

Many years later, a new king decided that he would pray and deprive himself of food and comfort until Ganga agreed to come to Earth. Ganga looked down upon this king from her watery throne and she said, "Yes. I will come. But remember, when I fall it will be with great force; the earth cannot hold my power."

The god Shiva heard this. "I will bear the goddess' fall," he said. "I will receive her on my head and protect the earth from her force."

With that, the sacred waters gushed from the skies. Ganga poured down on Shiva's tangled hair and she fell in rushing streams, over the mountains and across the earth. Fishes and turtles appeared. Porpoises flashed through the heavens, and white foam flecked the clouds.

From their elephants and chariots the gods and devas and demons watched the wondrous sight. Ganga fell now in a narrow stream, now in a broad torrent, down from heaven to Shiva's head to the earth. And as she flowed, all the creatures hurried to her side to touch her sacred purifying waters.

When she reached Ocean, where the sixty thousand sons had dug deep, she plunged in, and her waters washed the ashes of the sons of Sagara. At last they were cleansed, and their spirits could ascend to heaven.

Brahma said, "Ganga has come to Earth to be the sacred River Ganges. She shall endure as long as Ocean's waters endure, purifying all who come to her."

Devi & The Buffalo Demon

High in the golden mountains where the gods abide, the great mother Devi, the most powerful goddess of them all, was meditating. Suddenly her tranquility was interrupted by a noisy clamor. The gods came to her in distress. "Oh Goddess, save us, protect us!" they implored.

"Why do you need protection?" Devi inquired.

"It's the dreadful buffalo demon, Mahisha. He's causing terrible trouble, and we can't stop him," one answered. "He brought our elephants into his palace, took ten million horses, and kidnapped the celestial nymphs for his own pleasure. He struck Ocean with his horn and now demands that Ocean give him all its gems. He uprooted the mountains and pounded them to dust. Only you, great Devi, can destroy him."

"I know of Mahisha, this demon king with the head of a buffalo and the body of a man," Devi said. "It is true; only I can slay him. Do not fear. I will find a way."

She raised one of her eight graceful arms to bless them, and the gods bowed and left, saying, "Thank you for your protection, Mother of the Universe."

Using her vast magical powers, Devi changed herself into a beautiful maiden. She waited, sitting serenely in a mountain garden. As she expected, Mahisha the buffalo demon came looking for her. He had heard about the maiden who sat among the sweet-smelling flowers, meditating, and he wanted to see her. When he peered over the garden wall and saw the maiden's calm beauty, he muttered to himself, "She will be mine."

He went to the maiden and ordered her to stop her meditation. "Hear of my grandeur," he boasted. "I am not the old man who appears before you, but the great buffalo, king of the demons. No hero is as mighty as Mahisha. I can assume any form, accomplish anything. I am here to take you away with me to be my wife."

The maiden listened. She smiled and said, "I have no wish to be your wife. I'm not going anywhere with you."

The old man shook his cane at her. "But I have many treasure houses and servants. I can give you whatever you want! If you won't agree, I will take you by force."

"That will never happen, Mahisha."

In a flash, Mahisha turned from an old man into his buffalo demon form and, bellowing, charged the Goddess, ready to attack. But the maiden was gone, and in her place burned a blazing fire.

Mahisha was furious. He swelled as big as a mountain and snorted and pawed the earth with his hooves. He was a fearsome sight.

The gods, who were watching from a distance, rushed to the fire and dropped their weapons beside it. The flames shifted, changed shape, and faded, and out stepped Durga, the warrior side of Devi. She wore red armor, and in her eight hands she held a spear, a sword, and the other weapons the gods had brought to her. She called her lion to her side.

Durga mounted the lion and, in a voice like thunder, said, "I am Durga, the warrior who destroys all evil! Beware, buffalo demon!" Her terrible energy filled the skies like a rushing wind. The angry buffalo demon tossed mountains with his horns. He lashed the ocean with his tail so that it overflowed on all sides. His sharp horns pierced the clouds into fragments. The universe was in an uproar.

The goddess hurled a rope over Mahisha, and he quickly changed himself into a lion. With her sword she sliced off the lion's head. The demon appeared as a man with a sword and shield, prancing and taunting her. Durga drew her bow and pierced the man with her arrows, and he became a huge elephant, attacking Durga's majestic lion with his trunk. The goddess cut off his trunk, and once again the demon king assumed his buffalo shape. Puffed with pride at his strength and ability to change at will, he hurled mountains at the goddess. The earth shook.

"Roar, you fool," she called. "You will not roar for long. The end has come for you, buffalo demon!" With that she leaped from her lion to the buffalo's back and struck his neck with her foot. As soon as her ferocious power touched him, Mahisha's demon spirit rose from the mouth of the buffalo. As the demon came out, fighting, Durga hacked off his head with her sword, and the wicked Mahisha fell, slain at last.

Every creature in the world shouted with joy. The gods sang songs of praise to Devi and her war side, Durga. Ocean calmed, the mountains were still, and all the celestial nymphs danced in gratitude to the goddess.

DO UNTO ALL MEN
AS YOU WOULD WISH
TO HAVE DONE
UNTO YOU

Islam

42

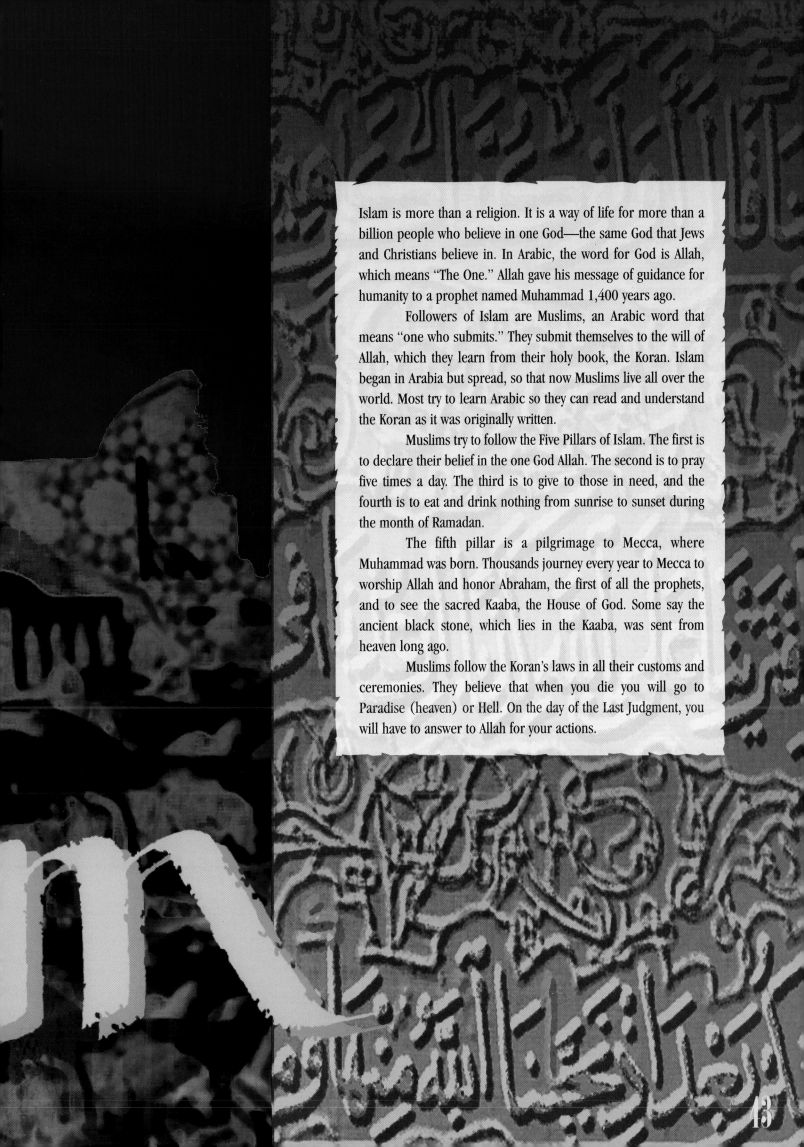

Islam is more than a religion. It is a way of life for more than a billion people who believe in one God—the same God that Jews and Christians believe in. In Arabic, the word for God is Allah, which means "The One." Allah gave his message of guidance for humanity to a prophet named Muhammad 1,400 years ago.

Followers of Islam are Muslims, an Arabic word that means "one who submits." They submit themselves to the will of Allah, which they learn from their holy book, the Koran. Islam began in Arabia but spread, so that now Muslims live all over the world. Most try to learn Arabic so they can read and understand the Koran as it was originally written.

Muslims try to follow the Five Pillars of Islam. The first is to declare their belief in the one God Allah. The second is to pray five times a day. The third is to give to those in need, and the fourth is to eat and drink nothing from sunrise to sunset during the month of Ramadan.

The fifth pillar is a pilgrimage to Mecca, where Muhammad was born. Thousands journey every year to Mecca to worship Allah and honor Abraham, the first of all the prophets, and to see the sacred Kaaba, the House of God. Some say the ancient black stone, which lies in the Kaaba, was sent from heaven long ago.

Muslims follow the Koran's laws in all their customs and ceremonies. They believe that when you die you will go to Paradise (heaven) or Hell. On the day of the Last Judgment, you will have to answer to Allah for your actions.

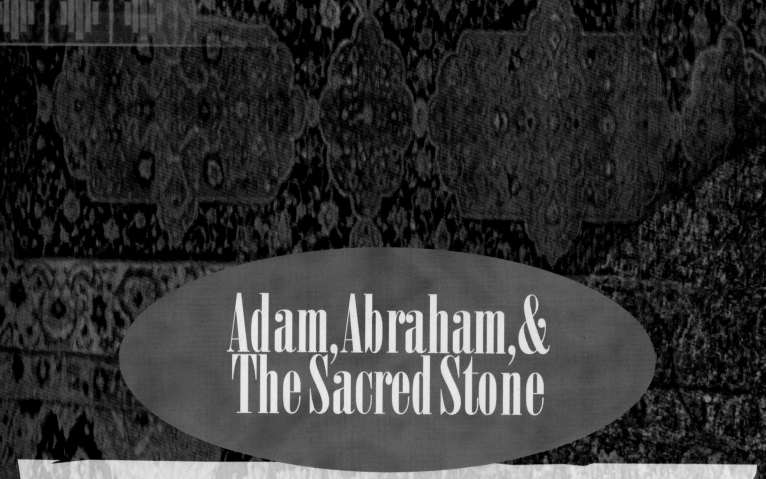

Adam, Abraham, & The Sacred Stone

Many years ago, when the world was new, Adam was wandering through Arabia. He and Eve, the first people, had been ordered from Paradise because they disobeyed God (Allah), and now Adam was looking for a very special place. God had told him to find the center point of the earth and there to build a Kaaba, a house of worship that would be dedicated to God.

Adam searched until he came to a valley surrounded by mountains. On a hill in the valley was a big white stone, shining in the sun. Adam knew it was a sacred stone. He said, "This is the place for the Kaaba."

The first man gathered stones from the nearby mountains and began to build near the shining white stone. Sweating in the heat, tired from the hard work, Adam kept on until he had completed the Kaaba.

The years passed. Adam and his family grew old and died. Gradually the Kaaba disappeared, covered by desert sands and a huge flood. One day the great prophet Abraham came, with his wife, Hagar, and their son, Ishmael, to the valley of the hidden Kaaba. Allah spoke to Abraham. He said, "I want you to leave Hagar and Ishmael here, Abraham. They will come to no harm."

Abraham obeyed Allah's will and left the valley. Hagar and Ishmael had only a few dates and a bottle of water, and soon these provisions were gone. Hagar was frantic. How would she care for her son? "Help me, oh God!" she cried.

She settled Ishmael to sleep in a safe, shady spot and ran to the hill of Safa, looking for water. She found not even a trickle. She ran to Mount Marwa. Again, no water. Seven times she ran back and forth, in desperate search of a lifegiving stream.

Hagar returned, weeping, to the place where Ishmael lay. What would become of them? Through her tears, she saw an angel.

"Why do you weep?" the angel asked.

"I am so thirsty, and there is no water for my child," she said.

The angel touched the ground with his wing, and Hagar heard a gurgling sound, like rushing water. On the spot the angel's wing had touched, pure fresh spring water was flowing.

Hagar thanked Allah with a grateful heart. She and Ishmael drank, and she began the work of making a home. Wandering herdsmen came through, and she allowed them to water their animals at the spring. In exchange they gave her sheep and goats. Hagar and Ishmael prospered.

Years later Hagar died and Abraham returned to the valley to be with his son. From the ruins of Adam's house of worship, on the same spot, the two of them rebuilt the Kaaba. When it was done, Abraham said, "Ishmael, do you see that great black stone on the hill?"

Ishmael shaded his eyes and squinted. "Yes, Father," he said. "I see it."

"That is a sacred stone. Once it was white, but man's sins have turned it black. We will place it in the Kaaba and pray to Allah to send a messenger who will guide the people to come."

And so they did, and the Kaaba and the sacred stone still stand in the town of Mecca.

Muhammad, Messenger Of God

Long ago, about 1,400 years ago, a child was born in a town called Mecca, in Arabia. He was named Muhammad. One day that name would be known around the world.

Before the child was born, his father died, and Muhammad's mother died when he was only six years old. The boy went to live with his grandfather and later his uncle, Abu Talib, and his aunt, Fatima. They all treated him with kindness and taught him to be a good person.

When he was grown, Muhammad became a camel herder and trader. He was poor and could not read or write, but he was known for his honesty and fair dealing.

A wealthy widow, a business woman named Khadija, heard about Muhammad and his reputation. "I need an honest man to work for me," she said, and so she hired him. She soon learned to trust and admire the young Muhammad. Khadija was forty years old and Muhammad only twenty-five, but age did not matter. They were married and lived happily together for many years.

In the valley of Mecca, the people worshipped and made sacrifices to many gods. Muhammad worried about this; he believed in only one god, Allah. He often went alone to a hill-top cave to meditate and pray.

One important day, when Muhammad was praying in the cave, he heard a voice. "Read," the voice said. Muhammad peered into the shadows. He saw no one. "I cannot read," he said.

"Read," the voice commanded. Now Muhammad was frightened and confused. "I cannot read," he said.

The voice spoke again. "Repeat after me, in the name of the Lord who created man from a clot of blood: the Lord is the most beneficent, who taught men what they did not know."

Muhammad said the words and ran from the cave. He looked toward the sky and there was a shining angel. "Muhammad," the angel said, "I am Gabriel, and you are chosen to be the messenger of Allah."

Muhammad couldn't believe his ears. He hurried home to Khadija and told her what had happened. "My dear, rejoice!" she said with a smile. "Allah has called you to be his messenger!"

From then on, Muhammad recited and preached the messages brought to him by the angel Gabriel. These commands to honor only Allah became known as the Koran, the holy book of Islam.

First a few people, then gradually more and more listened to Muhammad's preachings and became his followers. But some didn't believe his words. "We don't want to change our ways," they declared. Muhammad and his followers, obeying Allah's command, went to another place, Medina, where many people gathered to learn from Allah's messenger.

In the twenty-second year of his preaching, Muhammad wanted to go on a pilgrimage to Mecca. Non-believers said, "No, you cannot go to Mecca," and they sent soldiers to fight Muhammad and his followers.

The soldiers lost the battle. Muhammad returned to Mecca, and there the people said, "Now we truly believe. We will help to destroy the idols in the Kaaba, our ancient shrine, and dedicate it to Allah." And so they did.

The Miraculous Night Ride

One night, while Muhammad was sleeping, he suddenly wakened, sensing that something or someone was in the room with him. "Who is it?" he wondered. He looked up and saw, standing before him in the form of a man, the angel Gabriel. The angel beckoned. Wide awake now, Muhammad followed him outside. There he saw such a strange sight he thought he must be dreaming: it was a beautiful white horse, with wings sprouting from its sides. But it was not a dream.

The angel told Muhammad to climb onto the horse's back. They were going on a miraculous journey. Muhammad, the horse, and the angel Gabriel flew far through the night to the great city of Jerusalem. All the prophets—Adam, Noah, Abraham, Moses, Jesus—were waiting for them. At the Dome of the Rock, they all prayed together, and Muhammad was offered a choice of wine or milk to drink. He chose the milk. Gabriel approved. He said, "You have done the right thing, Muhammad. Wine is forbidden."

A magnificent ladder of light appeared, stretching high into the heavens. Muhammad knew he should start climbing it. Rung by rung, up the dazzling ladder he climbed, until he reached the gates of heaven. He was welcomed with joy by thousands of angels—all except one, who did not seem as happy as the others. "Why is he not smiling like the other angels?" Muhammad asked.

"He never smiles," Gabriel said. "He is Malik, the Keeper of Hell."

Muhammad said, "Will you order him to show me Hell?"

"Certainly," Gabriel answered, and he did so. Malik snatched the covering from Hell, and flames blazed high. Muhammad could see the unbelievers being punished for their bad actions.

He turned away and continued to climb the miraculous ladder, higher and higher past all the levels of heaven to the seventh level. He saw huge crowds of angels passing through the seventh gate. Gabriel told him, "Seventy thousand pass through here every day."

Muhammad noticed a man seated on a throne by the gate. "Who is that?" he asked, pointing to the man. He stepped closer and recognized Abraham, the ancient prophet and patriarch. As Abraham welcomed him into Paradise, Muhammad's vision ended. He was back in his bed at home.

A Boy Of Courage

Centuries ago, in ancient Medina, there lived a clever boy who was famous for his archery. He was so skilled with his bow and arrows, and his aim was so good, he could shoot a cluster of dates from the top of a palm tree or a pebble on a distant boulder.

Salamah, for that was the boy's name, was famous for something else, too—he was a great runner. In every race Salamah beat the other boys, and he often outran grown men. Once he even ran faster than a horse! But Salamah was best known for his devotion to Islam and Muhammad. He would do anything to please the blessed prophet and show his love of Islam. The fleet-footed boy would run errands for Muhammad, and as he passed by, people would say, "There goes Salamah. He can run as fast as a horse."

One day Salamah was out in the hot, dry hills near Medina, practicing with his bow and arrows, when he heard a commotion. He ran to the top of the nearest hill and looked down at the field where Muhammad's camels had been taken to graze.

The camels weren't grazing peacefully now. Several men on horseback were shouting at them and chasing them out of the field.

"They're stealing the prophet's camels!" Salamah exclaimed. He dashed down the hill and up another, looking for help. He saw a group of Muslims at work on the edge of town. "Help!" he called. "Hurry! Thieves are stealing the blessed prophet's camels!"

As soon as he knew they had heard him, Salamah turned to go after the thieves by himself. He ran like the wind, and soon he could see the thieves and the stolen camels, their hooves raising great clouds of dust on the road. Salamah ran closer, his heart pounding. He jumped behind a big boulder, placed an arrow in his bow, and prayed, "Allah, guide my arrows and do not let these men find that I'm alone."

He shot arrow after arrow at the camel thieves, so rapidly that they were afraid an army of Muslims had come after them. But the leader spotted Salamah, hiding behind a rock.

"It's only a child! Are you afraid of one young boy?" he shouted at his men.

Wheeling their horses around, they dashed after Salamah, furious because they had been tricked. In their anger they forgot all about the camels and wanted only to catch the boy who had dared to shoot at them. But Salamah had started to run the moment the leader saw him. He ran faster than he had ever raced in his life, with the bandits galloping behind him. Closer they came, and closer, as Salamah ran up a hill. Spying a clump of trees at the top of the hill, he dived into it and without a pause aimed an arrow. "If I can keep them back for a little while, help will come," he thought. "Allah be with me!"

The camel thieves circled and looked for a way to reach the boy, but they couldn't get past the arrows that shot like magic from his bow. He yelled at the bandits, hoping to keep their attention on him and away from the camels. "You'll never catch me!" he taunted. "If I run after any of you, you won't get away!"

His scheme worked. The angry bandits darted back and forth, up toward the trees and away again when the well-aimed arrows hit their mark.

The minutes began to seem like hours to Salamah. His arms were growing tired, and he only had a few arrows left. Just as he began to wonder if the Muslims were ever going to arrive, he saw them in the distance, riding fast. They dashed right into the group of thieves, swinging their swords.

The boy watched as the men on horseback fought fiercely. Blood flowed, and the bandits saw that they could not beat the Muslim defenders. Those who could escape turned and rode away.

"Salamah has saved the prophet's camels! Allah be praised!" the Muslim men shouted, and they trotted off to herd the camels home again.

That night all the Muslims in Medina gathered to praise the courageous boy who had tricked the bandits and saved Muhammad's precious camels. "This story will be told for generations to come," they said. Salamah would always be remembered for his bravery, his cleverness, and his love of Allah and the prophet Muhammad.

The Dog At The Well

One day Muhammad told his friends and followers a story about a thirsty man, a well, and a dog. This was the story:

A man left his home to take a long journey. It was a hot day, and he had not walked far before his head began to ache and his mouth felt dry. The sun blazed overhead, the fields he passed were brown and withered, and no water could be seen.

"I'm so thirsty. I must find water," he muttered. "Surely I will soon come to a well."

Just as he had the thought, he saw a well by the side of the road. Thankfully, he hurried to it, almost tasting the sweetness of the cool water that lay in its depths. But when he peered into the well, he saw no water. The well was dry. Disheartened, and even more thirsty now, he continued along the scorching road, hoping to find another well. Sure enough, before long he saw one. "At last, water!" he whispered, looking into the well. But it too was dry.

There wasn't a drop of moisture in the land. With a parched throat and feeling weak, the man walked on. "I can't go much further without water," he thought. And then he saw a well. Almost afraid to hope, he looked over the edge. Far below, in the darkness, water sparkled.

"Allah be praised!" the man said. He looked around for a rope and bucket to lower into the well so he could bring up the lifegiving water. There was no rope, no bucket. How could he reach the water he needed so badly?

Only one way remained. If the water would not come up to him, he would have to go down to it. He scrambled over the top and carefully, bracing himself against the sides with his arms and feet, descended into the well. Deeper and deeper he went, until at last he touched the cool, wet water. Cupping his hands, he scooped the water and drank and drank. He murmured, "Praise Allah for the liquid of life."

Feeling much better, the man began the long, difficult climb up out of the well. At last he reached the top and stood again on the road under the hot sun. He was starting to walk away when he heard a sound—a soft, sad whine. He looked down and saw a dog, sniffing at the ground. The dog looked miserable. His eyes were glazed, and he was panting with thirst. He came up to the man and licked the edge of his robe, which was wet from the trip down the well.

"This poor animal is as thirsty as I was," the man thought. "He'll die in this heat if he doesn't get water."

The dog looked up at the man and wagged his tail, grateful for the bit of moisture.

The man made his decision. "Wait here," he said. "I will bring you some water."

Into the well he went. Again he descended down, down, all the way to the bottom where the cool liquid lay. When he got there, the man braced himself against the walls of the well and took off his soft leather boots. He dipped one boot and then the other into the water and filled them. He clamped the tops of the boots between his teeth and began to climb up again.

This time the trip to the top was much harder. The heavy, water-filled boots pulled on his mouth, and his teeth hurt. Once the slick, wet leather slipped, and he almost dropped the boots, but he tightened his grip and held on. Slowly he kept climbing until he reached the top.

When he was on the ground again, he knelt and opened the boots so the dog could drink. The dog drank all the water in both boots, his tail wagging happily.

The man smiled. "Now neither of us will die of thirst," he said. He pulled on his damp boots, patted the dog again, and continued on his way.

Allah was pleased by this kind act. He was so pleased that all the man's past sins were forgiven, and years later, when the kind man died, his soul was taken to heaven.

The blessed prophet Muhammad concluded his story by saying, "You too will be rewarded for being good to all living creatures."

WHAT YOU
YOURSELF HATE
DO TO NO MAN

JUDAISM

Today Jewish people live all over the world, but their history began about 4,000 years ago in the region we now call the Middle East. Their first leaders and prophets were nomads in these countries. One of the three patriarchs, or fathers, of Judaism (and of Islam), was Abraham. He believed that there was one supreme being, one God, who created the universe and everything in it. This God is a non-physical, undefinable spirit.

Abraham's son, Isaac, and his grandson, Jacob, were the other patriarchs who led the Jews. Long after Abraham came Moses, a great prophet and teacher. Moses received teachings from God, which are called the Torah, and led the Jewish people out of Egypt and into Israel.

The Torah is the name for the first five books of the Bible, which to Jews and Christians alike is the sacred word of God. Another important book is the Talmud, which tells customs, rules, and stories. The Midrash is a book that explains Bible stories and gives advice for living a good life.

The God of the Jews listens to prayer and expects his followers to love him and obey his commandments. Some of the commandments are to worship no other gods, not to kill or steal, to honor your father and mother, and not to be devious. Some Jews believe that some day God will send a leader, called a Messiah, who will bring lasting peace to the world. Many others say that human actions will bring a Messianic age of peace.

Jewish people meet to worship in synagogues or temples. At home, they have a special ceremony on Friday evening and rest on the next day, the Sabbath.

Judaism has several celebrations during the year, each one a holy time that honors events in Jewish history. Rosh Hashanah, the new year, is in the fall; after it comes Yom Kippur, the most solemn holy day, for fasting and prayer. A day of joy in spring is Passover, celebrating the escape of the Jews from slavery in Egypt.

Adam & Eve In The Garden Of Eden

In the beginning, God created Heaven and Earth. In five days, he made the world and everything in it—the light and the dark, the earth and rivers and plants. On the sixth day, he made animals, and from the dust on the ground he created a man: Adam. Into Adam's nostrils God breathed the breath of life.

"I give all that I have made to you," God said. He saw what he had made, and it was good. On the seventh day he rested.

God put Adam in a beautiful garden filled with trees, a garden called Eden. He said, "Adam, you may eat fruit from any tree in the garden except one. It is the tree of the knowledge of good and evil. If you eat from it, you will die."

He brought all the creatures of the world to Adam, and the first man named them all. Lions and lizards, rabbits and ravens, cows and crows, aardvarks and zebras were given their names. Still, Adam had no human partner, and he was lonely. So God made him fall into a deep sleep, and while Adam slept, God took one of the man's ribs and from it made another person.

When Adam awakened, he was glad and he said, "She shall be called woman, because she was taken out of man." Her name was Eve, and they were husband and wife.

A sly serpent lived in the garden. He came to Eve and asked her if she could eat every fruit in Eden. "Yes," she said, "except for the tree in the middle. God said if we eat from it, we will die."

The snake said, "You will not die. God told you that because he knows that if you eat the fruit you will understand good and evil, and be as gods yourselves."

Eve saw that the tree was pretty, and she wanted to be wise. So she picked the fruit and ate it and gave some to Adam, and he ate too. They looked at each other and for the first time felt ashamed that they were naked, and they sewed fig leaves to cover themselves.

In the cool of the day, God walked in the garden. Adam and Eve were afraid and hid among the trees. God called out, "Adam, where are you?"

Adam came out and said, "I heard your voice, and I was afraid because I was naked, so I hid."

"Who told you you were naked?" God asked. "Did you eat from the tree I commanded you not to touch?"

Adam said, "The woman gave me the fruit to eat."

"What have you done?" God said to Eve.

"The serpent tempted me, and I ate the fruit."

God turned to the serpent in anger. "Because you did this, you are cursed above all other beasts. Upon your belly you will crawl, and you will eat dust all the days of your life."

To punish Eve he said, "I will multiply your sorrow and pain, and your husband shall rule over you."

He said to Adam, "Because you listened to Eve and ate of the tree, you shall eat in sorrow all of your life. You will work and sweat until you die and are in the ground, for dust you are and to dust you shall return."

God gave Adam and Eve animal skins to wear and said, "You know good and evil. Now lest you also take from the tree of life and live forever, you must leave the garden."

So he sent Adam and Eve from Eden, and at the eastern gate he placed angels to guard it and a flaming sword to protect the tree of life.

The Great Flood

God was angry. The people he had created from dust had become evil, and he was sorry he had ever made them. The earth was corrupt and filled with violence. In his wrath God said, "I will destroy man and beast, the creeping things and fowls of the air."

Except for Noah. Noah and his wife and his three sons and their wives respected God's will and did good, not evil. God said that they alone would be saved.

He told Noah to build a huge wooden boat, an ark big enough to hold Noah's family and two of every kind of animal, and food for them all. "Build an ark, Noah, because I will bring a flood of water," God said, "and it will rain for forty days and forty nights, and everything that is in the earth shall die."

Noah did as God ordered. When the ark was built, Noah and his family and the animals, two by two, went into the ark.

The rain fell. It poured night and day without stopping, and fountains under the sea broke open and spilled water over the land. Soon the hills and the mountains were covered. Everything on earth was drowned and destroyed.

Noah and his family and the animals were safe, floating in the ark. For 150 days there was only water as far as they could see.

Slowly, the waters began to recede. The ark came to rest on the top of a mountain called Ararat. Noah opened the window and sent out a dove, but she flew back. She found no place to rest.

The next week, Noah sent the dove out again. This time she returned with an olive branch in her beak. In another week he let the bird go again, and she did not come back. Now he knew the ground was dry and it was safe to leave the ark.

The people and birds and animals climbed out of the ark, and in gratitude Noah built an altar to God. God said, "I will never curse the ground again, never send another flood. This is my promise. I will place a rainbow in the clouds to remind me of my promise. While the earth remains, seed time and harvest, and cold and heat, and summer and winter, and day and night shall not cease."

Joseph & The Coat Of Many Colors

In the land of Canaan there once lived a good man named Jacob, who had a wife and twelve sons. They all worked hard in the fields and cared for the family's flock of sheep.

Jacob loved all his sons, but the youngest, Joseph, was his favorite. He doted on the boy, and the older sons were jealous of the attention their father gave to their brother.

On Joseph's seventeenth birthday, Jacob gave him a wonderful present—a beautiful coat, woven with designs and patterns in all the colors of the rainbow. Joseph was pleased with his new coat, but it made his brothers even more jealous.

"Why should he get such a fine present?" one complained. "I didn't get anything that nice on my birthday, or any other day."

Another said, "We work harder than he does. Father isn't fair."

When Joseph came near, the brothers walked away. Joseph ran after them. "Wait, brothers," he said. "I want to tell you about the amazing dream I had last night. It seemed so real. I dreamed that we were all out in the field tying up sheaves of wheat. My sheaf stood upright, and all yours bowed down to mine."

The brothers scowled. "So this means you, the youngest, will rule over us? Go away, Joseph. We don't want you around."

The next day, Joseph came to his brothers and said, "I've had another dream. In my dream, the sun, the moon, and eleven stars bowed down to me."

Now the brothers were really angry. Eleven stars bowing

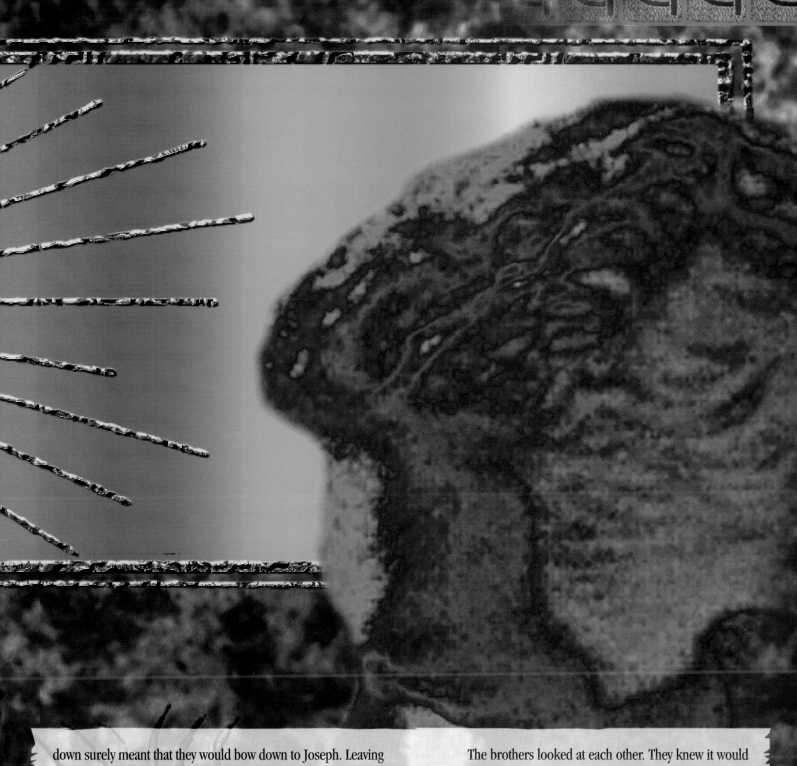

down surely meant that they would bow down to Joseph. Leaving him behind, they took the sheep to a far-off pasture.

Jacob was worried about his sons. "Joseph, go find your brothers and see if all is well with them and the sheep," he said. "Then come back and tell me."

Wearing his colorful coat, Joseph set off. He searched over hill and dale and through the fields, and finally he spotted them, feeding the sheep in a place called Dothan.

He called and waved, and the brothers saw him in the distance, his coat flashing purple and red and yellow against the blue sky.

One said, "Here comes the dreamer."

"I don't want him ruling over me," said another. "I wish he were dead."

The brothers looked at each other. They knew it would be easy to overpower Joseph and kill him. "Let's do it," they whispered. "We can kill him and throw him into a pit and tell our father that an animal attacked and ate him. We'll see what will become of his dreams."

The oldest brother disagreed. "We mustn't shed his blood, but we can cast him into the hole in the ground and leave him there," he said.

The others grumbled, but they followed his wishes. When Joseph reached their camp, instead of greeting him warmly, they surrounded him and held him down and stripped his coat away. They dragged him to the edge of the deep pit and threw him in. Joseph cried for help, but there was no one to save him.

Just then a group of men came riding by on camels. They stopped and greeted the brothers. One said, "We're headed for Egypt to sell our spices."

One of the brothers had an idea. He said, "We know how you can make more money. Buy our slave for twenty pieces of silver, and you can sell him to the Egyptians."

The traveling merchants agreed, and they pulled Joseph from the pit. The boy trembled in fear, but he didn't dare to say a word. His treacherous brothers turned their faces away as he was led into captivity.

After the camels and men were gone, the brothers killed a goat and dipped Joseph's coat in its blood. They carried it home to their father and told him they had found it.

Jacob wept and wailed in grief. "This is my son's coat; a beast has devoured him!" He refused to be comforted. He said, "I will go to my grave still mourning my beloved Joseph."

The brothers were remorseful and sorry they had caused their father such pain, but they didn't admit what they had done.

Jacob did not know that years later he would see Joseph again, when his son had become a powerful man, honored in Egypt.

Young Joseph started as a slave, but he won the trust of the Egyptian pharaoh, or king, by interpreting the pharaoh's dreams. "Your dreams show that Egypt will have many years when no crops will grow," he told the pharaoh. "You should build storehouses and save the grain while it is abundant."

The pharaoh ordered this done, and when the dry

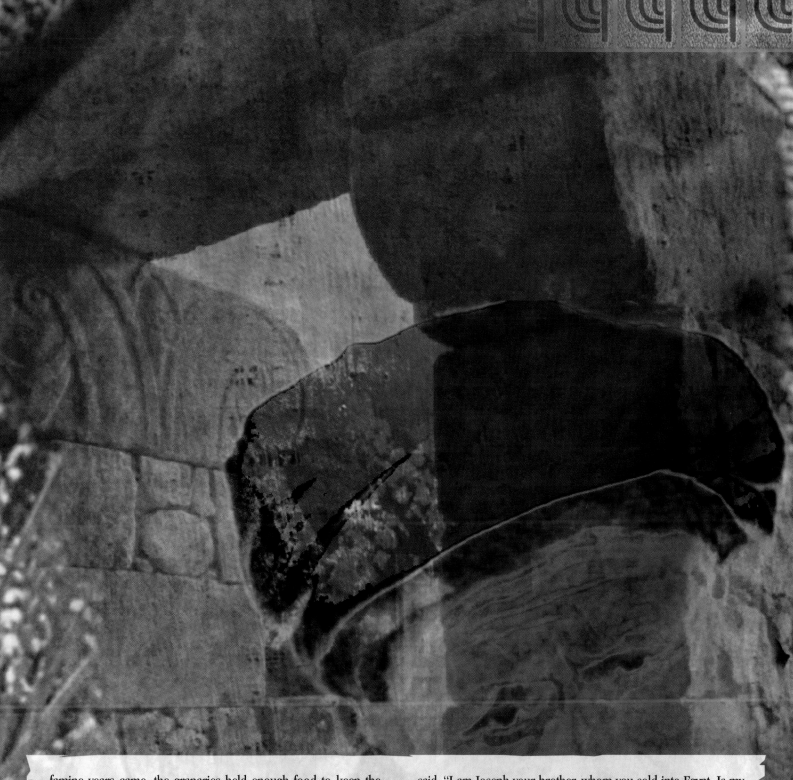

famine years came, the granaries held enough food to keep the people from starving. In fact, they held enough to sell to people in other lands where famine had struck.

One of those lands was Canaan, where Jacob and his family were going hungry. They had no food, but they knew that grain was stored in Egypt. "You must go to Egypt," Jacob told his sons. "Take money and gifts to the pharaoh and ask him for food in exchange."

The brothers set out for Egypt, never thinking that Joseph might still be alive. It was a long journey, but at last they arrived and bowed before Joseph, who was in charge of all the storehouses. They didn't recognize their brother, but he knew them and remembered his dreams of sheaves of wheat and stars bowing to him.

Tears came to Joseph's eyes. He reached out his arms and said, "I am Joseph your brother, whom you sold into Egypt. Is my father still alive?"

The brothers were speechless with amazement. Joseph, the brother they had almost killed years ago, here in the pharaoh's palace! Finally one said, "Yes, Father is alive and has never stopped mourning for you. Joseph, can you forgive us? We did a terrible wrong."

Joseph said, "Do not grieve or be angry with yourselves. It was not you who sent me here, but God. I was sent to help save people from starvation. So bring my father to me, and let us rejoice that we are together again."

The brothers were overjoyed. They gathered around him with love, thanking God, and they and their families lived near each other for the rest of their lives.

Moses In The Bulrushes

Many centuries ago, the pharaoh in Egypt forced the Hebrews into slavery. They were descendants of Jacob and Joseph, but this pharaoh did not care about that. He made the Hebrews work in the fields under the hot sun, form thousands of bricks from mud and straw, and build huge monuments and cities. They slaved all day, yet if they stumbled or their work slowed, they were whipped and sometimes killed.

Despite their misery, the Hebrews' numbers increased, and the pharaoh was afraid they might threaten his power. So he ordered his soldiers to take all the Hebrew baby boys and throw them into the Nile River.

The soldiers marched through the towns and into every Hebrew home. Distraught parents tried to protect their babies, but the soldiers were merciless.

One mother, determined to save her child, had an idea. She turned to her daughter, Miriam, and said, "We're going to give this baby a chance. Help me to weave a basket of reeds and seal it with pitch to make it watertight. I intend to set the baby in the basket and hide him among the bulrushes at the edge of the river."

"Mother, the basket will surely float away and my baby brother will drown," Miriam objected. Her mother sighed and said, "I have to try. We'll do what we can, and put our trust in God."

With nimble fingers, Miriam and her mother wove a basket and lined the inside with soft blankets. They tucked the sleepy baby into the basket and, in the dark of the night, crept away to the river's edge.

Like a little boat, the basket bobbed in the water, hidden from sight by tall bulrushes. Tears filled the mother's eyes as she bent to give her son a last kiss.

"I'm going to stay and watch over him," Miriam whispered.

"You're a good sister, Miriam," her mother said. "Be sure to stay well out of sight." She hugged her daughter and hurried home so no one would become suspicious.

Dawn came, and still the baby slept and Miriam kept watch, praying for the safety of her brother. All was quiet, except for the calls of the morning birds. Suddenly she heard laughter and women's voices nearby. Peering from behind a bush, Miriam gasped. It was the pharaoh's daughter! With her were her maidservants, coming to the river to bathe.

"Please don't see the basket," she prayed.

But the princess did spy the floating basket. She

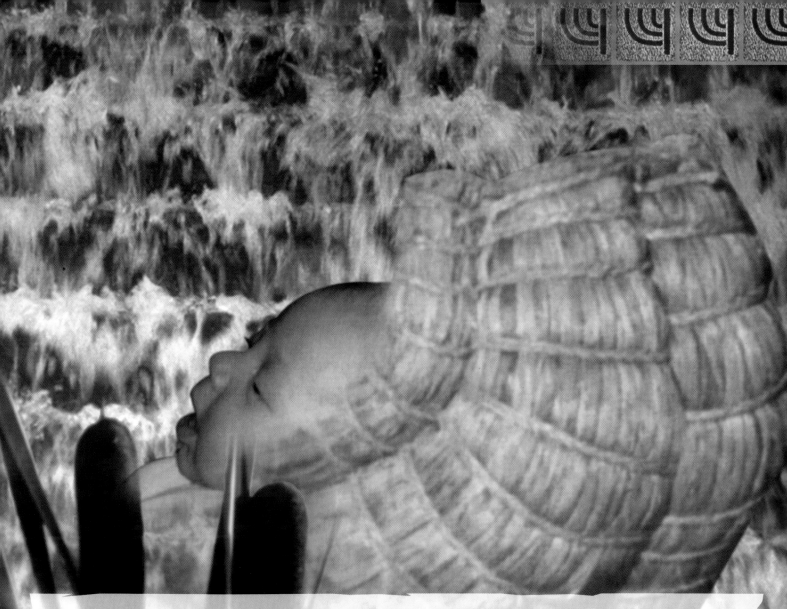

called to one of the maidservants, "What's that? Go out and bring it to me."

"Your Highness, it's a child," the maidservant said, as she dragged the basket to shore.

"A child! Yes, it's one of the Hebrew babies." The princess lifted the baby from the basket, and he wakened and began to cry. "Look, he's hungry." She cuddled him in her arms and tried to soothe him. "There, there, little one," she said. "I'd like to take you home with me."

Miriam took a chance. She stepped up to the princess and said, "Your Highness, shall I bring a Hebrew woman who has breast milk, so she can nurse the child for you?"

The pharaoh's daughter looked up and saw a girl in ragged clothing, with unkempt hair and dark, expressive eyes. She glanced from the girl to the baby and said, simply, "Go."

Miriam raced home, her heart pounding. "Mother, Mother!" she called the instant she stepped through the door of their mud-brick home. "God has saved the baby!"

Her mother was packing a meager lunch to take to work in the field. She stopped and stared. "What do you mean?"

Miriam's eyes danced with excitement. "You won't be going to the fields today. Come with me to the river. The pharaoh's daughter found the baby and wants to keep him. I told her I would bring a Hebrew woman to nurse him, and that's you!"

"Thank God," her mother said, and she and Miriam ran back to the river.

The baby was wailing now. The princess gave him to his mother. "Take this child and care for him," she said. "I will pay you. Bring him to me when he no longer needs nursing; I intend to raise him as my own son. He will come to no harm. I'm going to name him Moses, because I took him from the water."

Miriam and her mother took the baby Moses and returned to their home with joyful hearts, praising God.

When he was older, Moses was taken to the palace, and there, just as she had said, the pharaoh's daughter raised him as her own son. No one knew then that Moses would grow up to become a great Hebrew prophet. God had saved him from death so he could guide the Hebrew people out of slavery toward the promised land.

Long ago, in Israel, there was a shepherd boy named David. He was strong and brave and took good care of his family's sheep, protecting them from danger and leading them to grassy meadows. Sometimes he played soothing music on a little harp.

David had seven brothers. The three oldest brothers had left home to fight on the side of King Saul and the soldiers of Israel in a war against the Philistines. One day David's father said to him, "I am worried about my sons in battle. I want you to go to your brothers to see if they are well and take them corn and bread and cheese. You'll find them near the valley of Elah; I have heard that the soldiers are camped there."

Early the next morning, David left the sheep with a keeper and, with his bag of food, headed for Elah and the battlefield. Soon, in the distance, he could see the army camps. The Philistine men were on one hill and the men of Israel were on another, with the valley of Elah between them. Smoke rose from campfires, armor clanked, and the sun glinted on swords as the soldiers prepared for battle.

David searched through the crowd and found his brothers. They greeted him gladly and took the food. "Have you heard the news?" they asked.

"What news?"

The oldest brother said, "The Philistines have a great champion, a fierce warrior named Goliath who wants to fight someone from Israel. But no one is willing to go against the great Goliath."

"Look," a voice called. "Here he comes now!"

David craned his neck to see around the men who were staring across the valley. The camp was silent.

Goliath stood on the opposite hillside, holding a huge spear. He wore a helmet of brass and heavy armor. He looked as strong as an ox and as big as a bear. When he spoke, his voice boomed like thunder. "Hear me, armies of Israel! You cannot defeat the Philistines! Send one man to fight me. If he kills me, we will be your servants. But if I kill him, you will agree to serve the Philistines."

The soldiers looked at each other. They were afraid, and no one stepped forward. Someone said, "Whoever kills

David & Goliath

Goliath will be rewarded with riches by the king."

"But who could win in a fight against that giant? It isn't worth trying," another answered.

David cried, "This is an insult to Israel! Who is this man who defies the armies of the living God?"

His oldest brother turned in anger. "What do you know about it? You just got here. You are too proud. And who is taking care of the sheep you left so you could watch the battle?"

David turned away and went to the tent of the king. He bowed and said, "King Saul, I will go and fight the Philistine."

Saul was astonished. "You are only a youth," he said. "Goliath is a man of war. No one has ever beaten him."

David said, "Once a lion stole a lamb from my father's flock of sheep. I ran after him, and I killed the beast and saved the lamb. The Lord that delivered me from the paw of the lion will deliver me from the hand of the Philistine."

"Go then, and the Lord be with you," said Saul. He ordered armor for David and a helmet and sword. But David said, "No, I want only my shepherd's staff and five stones from the brook."

With the stones in his bag and his staff and sling in his hands, he set out to meet the giant. When Goliath saw David scrambling up the hill, he laughed scornfully. "Is this boy the best that Israel can do? Am I a dog, that you come with a stick? I will feed your flesh to the beasts of the field!"

"I come in the name of the Lord of Israel, whom you have defied," David answered boldly. To the watching soldiers, the shepherd boy looked very small as he approached Goliath.

But David was not afraid. He took a stone from his bag and put it into his sling, drew his arm back and threw with all his might. The stone sailed from the sling and hit Goliath in the middle of his forehead, and the giant fell to the ground with a crash. Instantly David rushed forward and pulled Goliath's sword from its sheath and cut off the warrior's head.

Amazed and frightened, the Philistine soldiers turned to flee, while the shouting men of Israel chased after them. Israel won the battle that day, and King Saul honored David and made him the leader of his army.

LIVE IN HARMONY, FOR WE ARE ALL RELATED

NATIVE AMERIC

Native Americans have a long spiritual tradition based on reverence for nature. All creatures are seen as living examples of one great spirit that is everywhere and in everything. Each bird and animal and tree contain a part of that spirit and can bring understanding and wisdom to those who pay attention.

For thousands of years this was the way Native Americans saw the world, though it was expressed in many different forms in different regions and tribes. It wasn't called a religion; they had no word for religion, because spiritual life was so intertwined with daily life it could not be separated and called something else.

Then Europeans came, bringing their own religions, and everything in Native life changed. The old ways were discarded or forced out, except in a few places, where some held onto the traditional beliefs. Today many more Native Americans are going back to the ways of their ancestors. Their special ceremonies, dances, drumming, regalia, stories, and chants are all connected with their spiritual lives.

In sweat lodges they purify their bodies and minds and feel the energy and power of Mother Earth and the Creator. On vision quests, they go alone into the wilderness to find self-understanding.

A Native healer and spiritual guide is called a medicine man or medicine woman, or sometimes a holy person or a spiritual healer. When a medicine man or woman treats an illness, he or she works with the sick person's feelings and thoughts, as well as the body. The healer, like everyone who follows the Native American path, believes that the way to have good health and inner peace is to take care of all parts of yourself and to respect nature and the community.

Grandmother Spider Brings The Sun

At the beginning of the world, there was only darkness. The animals stumbled around, tripping on roots and bumping into each other. "It's so dark here," they complained. "We need light."

Bear lumbered into a tree, rubbed his nose, and announced, "I have heard that there is light far from here. It's called the sun. But the people who have it won't share. Maybe we can take some from them."

"Good idea," Rabbit said, peering into the darkness. "Who will try to steal the sun?"

"I will," said Fox. He trotted off. He traveled for days and days, and finally he came to the place where the sun was. Softly he crept up, and when no one was looking, he snatched a piece of the sun in his mouth and ran away.

The sun piece sizzled in Fox's mouth. As he trotted along, he rolled it back and forth, and he licked it with his tongue, but nothing would cool it. It was so fiery hot, Fox dropped it and it fell beyond his reach. Even now foxes have black mouths, because Fox scorched his mouth carrying the sun.

"Let me try," said brave Possum. "I can hide a piece of the sun in my bushy tail." Away she went, traveling for days and days to the place where the sun was. Softly she crept up, and when no one was looking, she snatched a piece of sun and stuck it in her tail.

She started to run. She felt the sun burning the top of her tail, so she pushed it to the bottom. It burned that fur too, and soon all the fur on her tail was gone and the piece of sun slid off. Even now possums have hairless tails, because Possum burned hers carrying the sun.

"We are still in darkness. Who will bring us the sun?" Rabbit asked.

Grandmother Spider crawled up on her eight legs. "I will," she said. And off she went, traveling for days and days to the place where the sun was. Quietly she crept up, but in her wisdom she didn't try to hold the sun. Instead, she began to spin, and from the thread she wove a bag. With one swift move she snatched a piece of the sun, dropped it into her bag, and carried it back to the animals. They gathered around her in wonder and excitement. They could see the brilliant light and feel the heat that glowed through the bag.

"Where shall we put it?" Rabbit asked, his ears quivering.

Grandmother Spider said, "High in the sky, where everyone can see it and feel its warmth and light." But the tallest animals couldn't reach high enough to set the sun in the sky, even when they climbed the highest tree on the highest mountain.

"The birds!" Frog said. "The birds can take it into the sky. Buzzard flies the highest."

"Yes, yes, Buzzard!"

Grandmother Spider carefully placed her precious bag on top of Buzzard's head. His thick feathers would protect him from the sun's heat. Up he flew, carrying the bag higher and higher. The higher he went, the hotter the sun grew, until it was burning through the bag.

Still Buzzard kept flying upward. The sun burned through the bag and began to burn away the feathers on his head. The bare skin burned red. But Buzzard kept on until he reached the top of the sky. He shook his head, and the sun tumbled off and took its place in the sky, shedding light and heat on the world.

Even now, buzzards have red heads with no feathers because Buzzard's head burned as he carried the sun.

71

How Coyote Got His Name

In the early days, there were no human people on Earth. Only rock people and plant people and winged people and animal people. But change was about to happen.

Spirit Chief called the animal people together from all over the world and told them, "A tribe of new two-legged people is coming soon. Before they get here, you must choose the name and the work you want for yourself and all your descendants. Come to my lodge tomorrow at dawn and I will give each of you an arrow of power. The first one there will get first choice and the most powerful arrow."

Coyote was excited. He wanted a proud name and important work. He was tired of being called Coyote the Trickster because he was always playing tricks on people. "I'll be the first one at the lodge in the morning," he bragged. "I'll get a powerful name and important work."

"Your name suits you," said his brother Fox. "I think you have to keep it. No one else wants it."

Coyote said, "No! I don't want it. Let someone else be the Trickster. I'm going to be Grizzly Bear and rule the four-legged people. Or maybe Eagle, to rule the flying people."

Fox scoffed. "You will never get up early enough to be there at sunrise."

"I'll be there," Coyote said. "I am going to stay up all night. Maybe I will be called Salmon and rule the fish people."

He strolled to his lodge and built a fire to help him stay awake. For hours he crouched by the fire, listening to Owl hoot and

Frog croak. Gradually his eyes grew heavy and he felt more and more sleepy. He took two small sticks and propped his eyelids open. But even though his eyes were wide open, he fell asleep.

The sun was shining brightly when Coyote wakened. He jumped up and ran to the lodge of Spirit Chief. No other animals were there. "I'm first!" he announced loudly. "I choose the name Grizzly Bear."

Spirit Chief said, "That name was taken at the first light of dawn. Grizzly Bear got the longest arrow."

"Oh. Then call me Eagle." Coyote's voice was not so loud.

"Eagle flew away when the sky was still streaked with red."

"Well, I choose Salmon." His voice was small.

"Salmon swam off with the name at sunrise," Spirit Chief said. "All the names have been taken but yours. No one wanted it."

Coyote sank to the ground by the blazing fire of the lodge. His face was sad, and Spirit Chief pitied him.

"Trickster is a good name for you. You are who you are. But you have important work, too. You will save the new two-legged people from monsters and teach them how to make fire, catch fish, and carry wood, and they will honor you for it. And you will have the power to change into any form you can imagine and to come to life again after you die."

Coyote felt much better. He puffed up his chest and off he went, looking for mischief.

Buffalo Woman's Gift

A very long time ago, two young warriors left their hunting group to scout for buffalo. Over the rolling green hills they went, through the tall grass, scanning the horizon, looking for game. They watched for the slightest movement that would tell them the mighty buffalo was near. At the top of a hill, one said, "I see something! There, in the north."

The other shaded his eyes with his hands and said, "I see it too. But it's not buffalo. There is something strange about it."

They watched in silence and wonder as a mysterious creature came toward them. The only sound they heard was the whisper of the wind rustling the grass.

"It's a woman," one scout said. "A young woman, with long shining hair."

The other scout spoke softly. "More than that, she is a holy being. She walks, but her feet do not touch the ground, and a bright light surrounds her."

The first one scoffed. "She's a beautiful woman, and she is alone. I can do whatever I want with her."

"This woman is sacred! Forget those bad thoughts."

But the first scout paid no attention. He swaggered toward the woman, who was dressed in the finest of soft white deerskin and carried a bundle on her back. When the man came close to her, she lifted her arms and suddenly a misty cloud rose out of nowhere and swirled around them.

Gradually the cloud blew away and the beautiful woman stepped forward. On the ground lay the skeleton of the foolish scout.

The man who had watched all this stood trembling.

To him she said, "You are the true warrior. You do not wish to harm those who cannot defend themselves, and you serve your people well. Go home now and prepare a tipi for me. Soon I will come with a gift that will bring harmony to all the people."

The scout ran back to the camp and told the people what had happened. "This woman has great power," he said, "and she is coming soon with a gift for us."

The people gathered poles and buffalo skins and built a big tipi. Dressed in their best buckskin clothes, they went into the tipi and sat down to wait with their chief, Standing Hollow Horn. The chief wore his ceremonial headdress of eagle feathers.

After a time the beautiful woman appeared, singing, and as she sang, white, sweet-smelling clouds came from her mouth. She entered the tipi. She stood before Standing Hollow Horn and pulled something from her bundle. The people stared. A pipe? Was a thing so ordinary the wondrous gift?

The woman spoke. "Behold the sacred pipe," she said, pointing the stem upwards. "It brings you a message from Grandmother Earth and Grandfather Sky. With this pipe they tell you to remember that all life is sacred, all life is connected. When you smoke the pipe in your ceremonies, it will help to show you the right road to follow."

She put the pipe in the chief's hands, and she said, "The pipe is made of stone and wood, representing Earth and all that grows upon it. The bison calf carved on the pipe is a reminder that Mother Earth feeds and cares for us and our four-legged relations and those that swim and crawl. The twelve eagle feathers that hang from the stem represent the sky and our brothers and sisters with wings. The smoke that breathes from the pipe is a prayer and thanksgiving for everything in the entire circle of life."

Singing again, the holy woman stepped out of the tipi. The people watched her go far across the prairie, and it seemed that suddenly she was no longer a woman, but a white buffalo calf, prancing and raising dust as she ran.

Later around the fire they shared the sacred pipe and thought of the Buffalo Woman's words, while the smoke, spiraling up and away, carried their prayers of thanks.

In the sky, high above the clouds, there grew a rare and beautiful tree. Delicious fruits and fragrant flowers hung in its branches, and its long white roots spread out and were rooted solidly in the four sacred directions.

One night the wife of the chief who lived in the sky dreamed that the huge tree was pulled out by its roots. She told the chief of her dream.

"This is a powerful dream," the chief said. "The spirits have told you that we have to uproot that tree."

He called in the young men, and they tugged and yanked at the tree, but they could not make it budge. And so the old chief himself grabbed at the tree with his mighty arms and pulled. Slowly, its roots creaking, the tree began to move. The chief strained and pulled harder, and finally the immense tree came up and lay on its side.

Clutching a branch of the toppled tree, the sky woman peered into the huge hole where the tree had been. "I see something shiny!" she said. As she leaned over to see better, she lost her balance, her hand slipped from the branch, and she fell. Some say she jumped because the blue world below was so beautiful.

Down, down, down, down she spun, with a handful of seeds from the branch still clutched in her hand. Far below her lay a vast expanse of water—nothing but glittering blue water.

In that water two swans were paddling about. One looked up and said to the other, "Something is falling out of the sky."

"It's a strange animal," the other said. "Let's go help it."

All the birds and fish and animals that lived in the water watched as the swans flew up and caught the falling woman on their wings and gently brought her down.

"This animal can't live here," the goose said. "She can't swim without webbed feet."

A water bird said, "She needs dry ground to stand on. Maybe we can bring her some from the earth that lies beneath the water."

Turtle Island

The duck, a good diver, said he would try. Down he dove, as far as he could beneath the water's surface, but he couldn't find the bottom. The beaver tried, and the loon. Neither could find earth.

"I'll go," said the muskrat.

"If I couldn't make it, you certainly can't," the beaver said with a sniff. "I'm bigger and stronger, and a much better swimmer."

"Let her try if she wants to," the swans said. They were still holding the woman who fell from the sky on their broad wings.

The little muskrat took a deep breath and dove. Through the dark water she swam and swam until she was tired and her breath was nearly gone, and still she kept swimming, down further and further. Finally she touched bottom. She grabbed a bit of earth with her paw, clenched it tightly, and let herself float upwards.

The other creatures were waiting anxiously. "There she is!" the duck said as the muskrat appeared, gasping for air.

The beaver said, "She didn't find earth."

"She did! She has some in her paw!"

"What are we going to do with it?" the loon wondered.

A voice spoke like the beat of a drum. "I will hold it on my back." It was the turtle, who had been watching and listening all the while.

The animals brought the exhausted muskrat to the turtle. The little animal opened her paw and dropped the bit of earth on the turtle's shell. Quickly, faster than the eye could see, the earth expanded and grew and grew until it became all the land in the world. The turtle blinked, but he didn't falter. He braced his sturdy feet and continued to hold the earth on his back.

The swans carried the woman to the land and set her down. She dropped the seeds she was still carrying from the great sky tree onto the ground. Immediately green shoots sprouted and plants began to grow.

From those seeds came the first trees and bushes, gifts to all the generations. The turtle holds it up, and in his honor the people call it Turtle Island.

Raven is in his boat, fishing, fishing at the mouth of the river. Fog Woman moves softly, spreading her gray cloak across the river, and sits in the boat. Raven says, his voice hoarse in the mist, "Who is there?"

Fog Woman whispers, "It is I, Raven. Why are there no salmon in your boat?"

"Because I cannot see to fish."

"Send your servants to fetch my baskets, there in the cattails, my cedar baskets woven with sky and clouds."

Raven says, "Do as she says," and the servants go in search of the baskets, the cedar baskets. They find them in the cattails and reeds on the riverbank, they find them and bring them to the boat.

Fog Woman takes the baskets, her woven cedar baskets, and gathers the fog. In huge handfuls she piles it, piles it into her baskets, and the sky turns blue again.

Raven laughs and stares with his hot yellow eye, and he casts his fishing line into the water. A salmon bites, and he pulls it in. He casts again and catches again, and again and again until he has many fish. Fog Woman watches, she holds

Raven & Fog Woman

her baskets and watches.

In camp on the bank of the river, the servants clean the salmon, they clean them and smoke them in racks by the fire.

"My salmon, mine," Raven says, and he preens his black feathers proudly. He struts in pride, in preening pride, and his wings brush against the racks and knock them down. The salmon, the good salmon falls into the sand.

Fog Woman sees Raven and the salmon on the ground, she sees them, and silently she takes her baskets and her fog and her salmon and disappears into mist.

"Come back!" Raven calls. "Come back with my fish."

Fog Woman is gone. She is gone.

Raven goes fishing in his boat at the mouth of the river. Fog Woman comes softly, softly, spreading her gray cloak.

"Fog Woman, gather your fog," Raven begs. "We are hungry, and we cannot see to fish."

Sometimes she hears, and she gathers her fog, she gathers it into her baskets. Raven fishes and fishes, and he always leaves the first salmon, the first one, for Fog Woman.

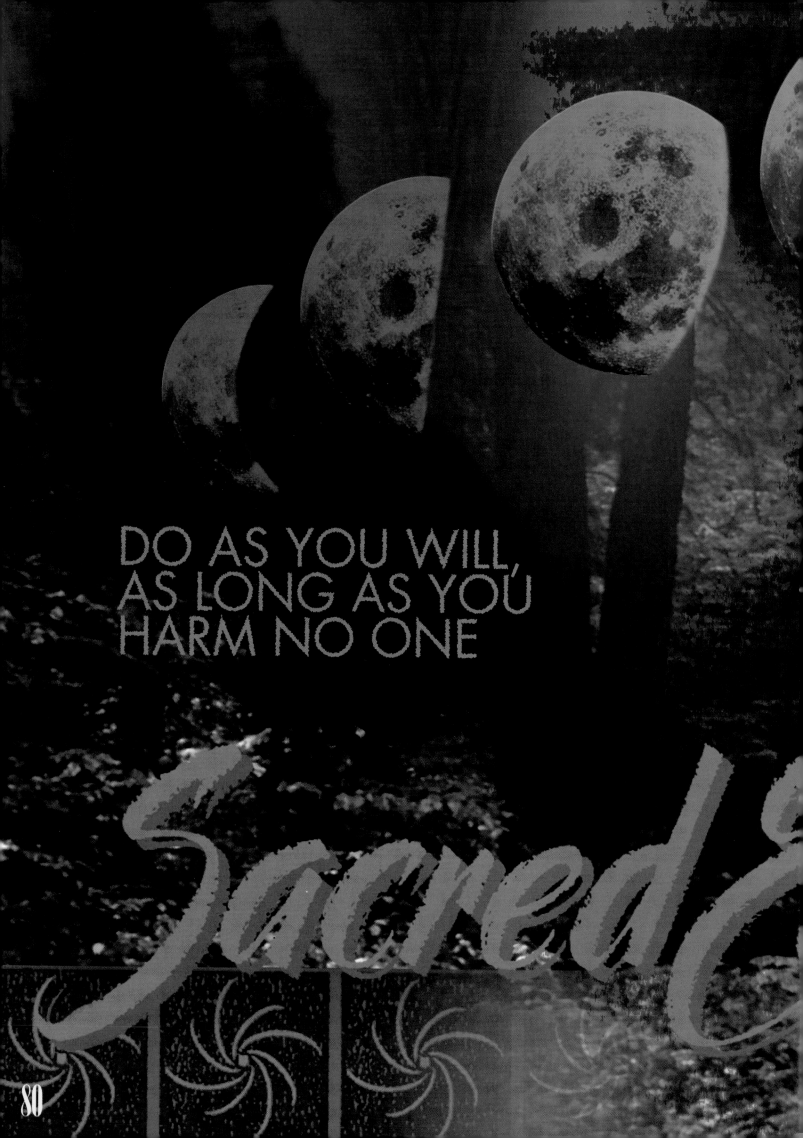

DO AS YOU WILL,
AS LONG AS YOU
HARM NO ONE

The Earth-centered movement that has developed in the late twentieth century has no set dogma, or group of religious teachings. There is no one name, either. These beliefs have been called Paganism, Neo-Paganism, Wicca, Goddess Religion, Eco-Feminism, New Age Spirituality, the Old Tradition, and many others.

They are all different ways of expressing a belief that everything in nature is sacred and should be treated with respect and love. They teach that you should not try to separate yourself from the rest of nature, but celebrate and appreciate your part in it.

They honor the seasonal and moon cycles and the greater cycles of the universe. Most people on the Sacred Earth path believe that when our bodies die, we continue to exist in some other form, as part of a vast, unending cycle. Goddesses and gods in these beliefs are honored as natural forces and the sacred spirit deep within us, not as rulers to be worshipped.

Some groups look back thousands of years to early nature-based religions for their rituals and spiritual vision. Others borrow from past and present-day religions and combine that wisdom with new ways. They say that spiritual knowledge is already in each of us, and we can discover it through meditation, ritual, and trying to live in cooperation with Earth and one another.

Some groups meet every month at the full moon, others when the season changes or at certain particular times. They may get together in a meeting hall, someone's home, or out in the woods or countryside. The often use candles, incense, music, and dance in the ceremonies to help discover and share spiritual awareness.

Occasionally, several groups will gather at big outdoor festivals for dancing, music, singing, chanting, sharing food, and honoring the gifts of Earth. The biggest celebrations are held on the days of the spring and fall equinox and the summer and winter solstice.

The myth of Demeter and Persephone in this chapter is a version based on the research done by Charlotte Spretnak and expressed in her book, *Lost Goddesses of Early Greece: A Collection of Pre-Hellenic Myths.*

Gaia Creates Herself

Out of the Great Nothing there exploded a thunderous sound, the music of all the sounds that ever were or will be, a sound so loud it pulsated for eons, and with the mighty sound came billions of chunks of fire and light and rock and dust, streaking across the wide emptiness.

One of the chunks was Gaia. She spun out and away, farther and farther, rolling and spinning herself into a ball. She tilted, she turned, she danced to the music and the rhythm of the sound. All around her, and in the farthest reaches of distance, fireballs glowed. The closest fireball bathed one side of her in light, while the other side rested in the cool, shadowy dark. As she spun, the dark side turned to light, and the light to dark. And so she spun, light and dark, light and dark.

She stretched and, still spinning, she spewed fire and rock and from her body came mountains, valleys, hills, ridges, plains, chasms. She breathed, and clouds formed, and rain fell, and deep oceans filled her sides, splashing against the shores. Rivers flowed through her valleys.

Gaia laughed, and life came forth. Fishes swam, green shoots sprouted, creatures walked over the contours of her body. Gaia was exultant. She loved what she had done. She couldn't stop! She laughed again, creating more and more life, just to feel it growing, flowing, swimming, crawling, breathing—ferns, moss, pterodactyls, dandelions, daisies, hemlock trees, giraffes, cocker spaniels, carnations, snakes, tarantulas, tigers, butterflies,

redwood trees. And humans.

Gaia, the Great Mother, laughed men and women into being, and they stood and walked in wonder on the soft green grass. They saw snowy mountains, a high blue sky, apple trees. They smelled pine needles and sun-warmed blackberries, heard the hiss of the surf and the croak of the raven, touched rough stone and soft skin.

Gaia provided clear water and abundant food for her creatures. In dreams and visions she came to the humans and taught them where to find plants they could eat, and roots and ripe fruits and berries. From her they learned to walk quietly in the forest and jungle and speak to the spirits of the animals they hunted for food and fur.

In her wisdom Gaia gave sorrow, for without it, humans cannot appreciate happiness. She gave joy, anger, curiosity, fear, grief, hope, and love. She was the provider of everything, of earthquakes, hurricanes, and floods as well as sunny days and gentle nights. She who created life and sustained it, took it back into her body after death.

The humans adored Gaia, the Great Mother, and revered her power. In gratitude for her gifts, they placed offerings for her in clefts in the rocks and earth. Sometimes they left honey and cakes, sometimes grain or fruits. Always they left their grateful thanks.

Gaia smiled and kept on spinning. And still she spins.

The Wheel Of The Year

At the darkest time of the northern year, when the tree branches are bare and the roots are resting in the ground, it is Yuletide, and Earth Goddess gives birth to a child. She rests, smiling gently upon her child, he who will bring back the sun. The people rejoice.

Gradually the days grow longer. The young god's Mother, the great Earth Goddess, rises from her rest. It is early spring, a time to celebrate the coming of light and fertile growth.

The god stretches and grows taller. The early buds swell and burst. Daffodils bloom yellow on the greening grass,

pussywillows fuzz on branches, and violets cover the meadows. The young god runs through the fields with joy. It is Eostra, when the hours of day and night are equal.

At Beltane, the god has grown to maturity. He is full of strength and energy, and the fields and forests are bursting with life. Seeds are sown in the fertile earth, and the Goddess is again pregnant. The people gather flowers and branches and decorate their homes in her honor. They dance around the ribbon-bedecked May-pole.

Now the powers of Nature are at their highest. It is the summer solstice, Litha, when all the roots and plants are busy

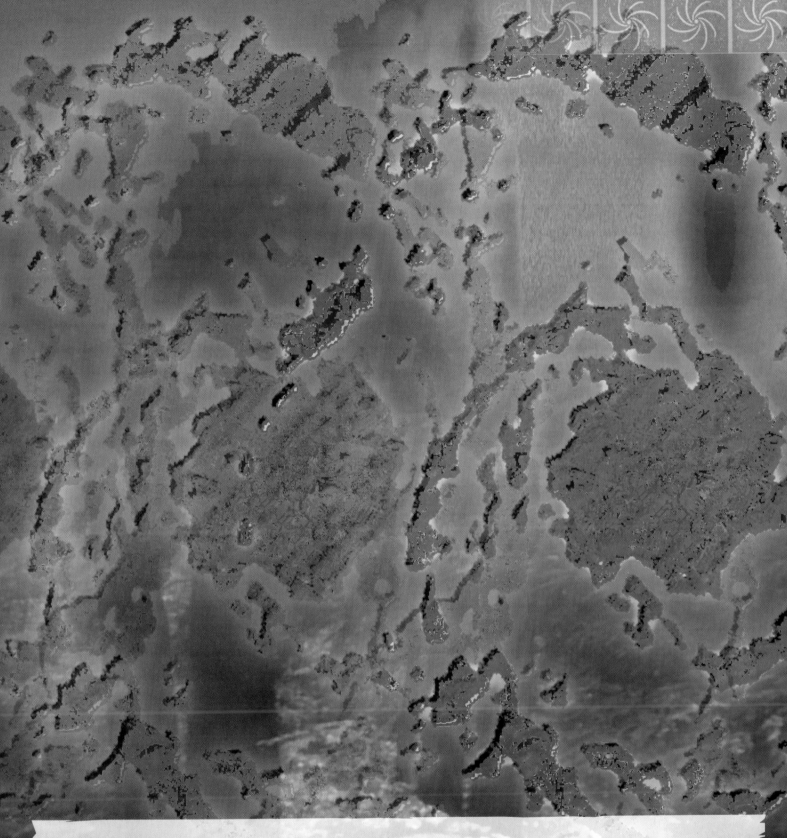

feeding and growing, the bees collecting pollen, the birds tending their young. The belly of the Goddess grows.

Soon comes the first harvest of summer. Even as the people reap their early crops, they see the sun rise farther in the south each day, and the god begins to lose his strength. The nights become longer. The people remember that change is constant, and they thank the goddess and god for every grain, every meal. They set food aside for the coming winter.

Autumn Equinox arrives and the harvest is complete. Day and night again are equal. The people hold feasts of thanks. The god prepares to die, which he must do to be reborn. Nature settles in for rest. The leaves fall, the creatures are tucked away in their dens.

The wheel of the year turns to All Hallow's Eve, and the people bid goodbye to the god. He has gone, and yet he is present, waiting within the goddess to be born. At this powerful time, when the veil between the worlds is thin, the people ponder the meaning of death and honor those who have gone before. The Goddess rests before giving birth to the god, and her people settle in for the dark time, knowing that Yuletide is on its way again.

The great wheel continues its majestic, endless circle.

Mella & The Python Healer

It was nighttime in an African village, and everyone was asleep. Everyone except Mella. The young girl had quietly slipped away from home and gone into the forest to a moonlit clearing. She had come to this sacred place to pray to the moon goddess.

Clutching the crescent-shaped gold amulet that hung on a chain around her neck, Mella looked up at the moon glowing high in the sky and whispered, "Oh, merciful Bomu Rambi, please help me. My father is ill, and all our medicines and music and magic have not healed him. I fear he will die. What shall I do?"

She waited, feeling the powerful presence of the goddess, until she heard Bomu Rambi's soft voice. "You must go to the Python Healer." The Python Healer! Mella's heart

quickened, and her body felt cold. Only a few months before, her older brothers had gone to the python's cave and returned shaking with terror, too frightened even to speak. Now she, a girl alone, was expected to face the great snake.

Mella hurried back to her village and home. She lay awake on her straw mat, listening to her father's groans of pain until the first light of day. Quickly she placed a few roots and grains in a small sack of elephant hide, and she set off toward the cave of the Python Healer.

For four days Mella walked, following paths made by the animals who lived in the warm, damp, earth-fragrant forest. She felt their eyes watching her as she passed by ferns as high as her head, crossed swift-moving streams, and made her way up and down rocky hills. When she thought of her

beloved father, she lifted her spirits by singing songs of hope. At night, when she was too tired to continue, the moon guided her to sheltered groves where she slept on moss and dreamed of Bomu Rambi.

Late one evening she came to the mountain cave where the python lived. She had never been so far from home. She stood at the entrance, and with her heart hammering in her chest, she called, "Python Healer, I am Mella, and I have come to ask your help. My father has been ill for a very long time. Please, will you send him your healing powers?"

The forest fell silent. Even the birds seemed to be waiting, and to Mella the time that passed felt longer than all the days she had walked. In the darkness of the cave she saw eyes glowing, and she heard a voice hiss, "Foolish girl, the

bravest of your people have fled in terror from my door. Do you not fear that I might strangle you and strew your bones about my cave?"

"It is not that I have no fear," Mella replied. "I come to you because my love is louder than my fear. My father has done no wrong, yet he lies dying and nothing can rid him of his illness. Bomu Rambi answered my prayer, and she sent me to you."

From the cave the voice hissed again. "Sssso, your love is more powerful than fear of me? Would you be willing to turn your back and let me crawl close to you?"

Head held high with the pride of her people, Mella turned her back to the cave and faced the shadowy forest.

"Sssso, you think your love is more powerful than

your fear of me?" The hiss was at her heels now. "Would you let me twine myself about you, as I might do if I chose to take you for my dinner?"

Mella took a deep breath and stretched out her arms. She felt the cool, thick snake slither around her feet and begin to wind itself about her body. When the many rings of the python were completely coiled around her, except for her head and hands and feet, the snake said, "Sssso, your love is more powerful than your fear of me? Take me to your home."

Mella held her head high, despite the weight of the huge serpent, despite her fear. Drawing upon all her courage, she began to walk, and as she walked she sang. The animals and birds of the jungle watched her pass by, and they growled and chirped their respect for the brave girl.

Back through the forest she walked, over the rocky hillsides and swift streams, until she arrived at the village with the Python Healer wrapped around her body. When the villagers saw this strange creature approaching, they ran for their spears. Mella called out, "Stop! It is Mella, inside the Python Healer! I am going to my father."

In her home, Mella's father lay thin and weak upon his mat. Slowly the serpent uncoiled itself and said to Mella, "Follow my instructions. Take the healing bark and oil from the pouch around my neck, and put them into a fire." The girl did so, and the vapors of the burning bark floated into the room. The Python Healer swayed and began to chant strange and holy sounds.

After a time, Mella's father opened his eyes, and he stretched and sat up. When he stood and smiled at her, Mella was filled with happiness and gratitude. Her father was well and strong again!

"How can I thank you enough?" he asked the serpent. "You and Mella have saved my life. Let me give you food and

drink, let us celebrate."

The Python Healer said nothing. Once again it began to coil itself around Mella's body, and she knew she would have to repeat the journey to the cave. Back to the mountainside she walked, and finally felt the python unwind itself from her exhausted body. As she turned to leave, the snake spoke. "Enter my cave."

Mella hesitated for only a moment, and then she stepped into the darkness. A tiny light glowed far back in the cavern. As she moved toward it she dreaded seeing the broken bones scattered over the ground, but to her astonishment, when she got to the light she saw sparkling jewels and piles of gold and silver. "Sssso, your love was indeed stronger than your fear," the Python Healer said. "I wish to reward you. Take what you desire."

Amazed, Mella said, "I cannot choose." With its mighty jaws, the python picked up a golden chain with a gold moon crescent hanging from it and brought it to Mella. It matched the one she always wore, the one she had touched to call upon Bomu Rambi.

"Thank you, Python Healer," Mella said, and she left the cave and returned to the village.

When her brothers heard about the python's riches, they plotted greedily to steal them. But Mella overheard their plans, and again she hastened to the cave, this time to warn her serpent friend. When the brothers arrived at the mouth of the cave, they were greeted with thunderous roars and billows of hot stinking smoke, and they ran away in fear.

Mella grew up to become a wise and beloved leader of her people. It was Queen Mella who ordered that a wooden figure be carved and placed in the center of the village—a figure of her friend, the trusted Python Healer, the one who understood courage and love.

Inanna In The Underworld

Goddess Inanna of Sumer was a great and glorious queen. In her long flounced robe of purple, wearing her high crown, she sat on her throne made from the huluppu tree. The head of a lion was on her scepter, and flowers grew from her shoulders. An owl stood by her side. Inanna ruled wisely, for Enki, the God of Wisdom, had given her the gift of wisdom. She made the rain fall and the grain grow in abundance; she delighted in sweet-smelling herbs and bright flowers.

When Inanna and her husband, the shepherd Dumuzi, united in passionate embrace, the harvest was bountiful and the fields fertile. She set Dumuzi on the throne and made him king.

Inanna knew all there was to know of Heaven and Earth, and now it was time to learn of the vast Underworld, where her sister Ereshkigal was Queen. Inanna turned to her priestess, Ninshubur. "My faithful friend," she said, "I am descending to the Underworld. If I do not return, go to the temple of Enki, the God of Wisdom. Enki will help me."

Ninshubur anointed the goddess's skin with scented oils and dressed her in fine robes and jewels. Alone, carrying her shining scepter, Inanna journeyed to the gates of the Underworld.

The gatekeeper said, "What do you want, Inanna?"

"I have come to see my sister Ereshkigal," Inanna announced.

The gate swung open. Inanna stepped in and the gatekeeper snatched away her crown. Quickly she turned to strike him with her scepter. "No, Inanna," he warned. "This is what you must do if you wish to descend to the Underworld."

He pointed the way, and she began to walk the downward, spiraling path. Soon she came to another gate. Again the gate opened. "Now you must give up your jewels," the gatekeeper said. Inanna hesitated, but she gave him her precious, sparkling jewels, one by one.

She continued down to a third gate. When it opened, the gatekeeper said, "Your scepter, Inanna."

She gave him the sacred scepter. The path descended before her. She walked to the next gate. This time she gave up her sandals. At each gate she surrendered another possession until, at the seventh gate, she unclasped her royal robe and handed it to

the keeper. Inanna had nothing left—no clothing, no crown, no scepter. She was deep in the dark Underworld.

A door opened, and Inanna entered a shadowy room. There stood Ereshkigal, tall and majestic, with the judges of the Underworld surrounding her. "Those who come here may not leave," they said, and Ereshkigal struck. Inanna's limp body was hung from a hook on the wall.

Meanwhile, the priestess Ninshubur waited. Three days and three nights went by, and Inanna did not return. Ninshubur wept and mourned, and she went to the temple of Enki. "Oh, save Inanna," she cried. "Enki, do not let the Queen of Heaven die in the Underworld!"

Enki scraped dirt from under his fingernails and formed two creatures. He gave them the food and water of life. "Go to the Underworld," he commanded. "Sprinkle Inanna's corpse with the food and water of life, and she will arise."

The creatures obeyed, squeezing through the seven gates of the Underworld. They found Inanna's body hanging on a hook and sprinkled the food and water of life over it, and Inanna arose,

whole again. Gratefully she turned to ascend from the Underworld. The judges stopped her.

"Even Inanna cannot leave here so easily. If you wish to leave, you must provide someone to take your place."

Inanna agreed and began the long return trip, collecting her royal garments and possessions as she passed through each gate.

Who would take her place? Ninshubur? "No," Inanna said. "Ninshubur is my faithful companion." She walked on. Her two sons? "No, not my dear sons. They care for me."

She came to the throne where her husband sat in glory, enjoying himself. Dumuzi was not grieving; he had forgotten her. Inanna ordered, "Take Dumuzi!"

Dumuzi's sister wept and wailed. "Take me instead!"

Inanna pitied her. "Because you have asked," Inanna said, "Dumuzi will go the Underworld only half the year. You may take his place for the other half. So it will be."

And once again the radiant Goddess of Heaven and Earth sat upon her throne.

Demeter & Persephone

Long long ago, far back in the mists of time, flowers bloomed all year round, and the leaves on the trees were always green. Grain and olives, fruits and vegetables grew and ripened, were picked and eaten, and grew again. Rain fell gently, and the sun shone warm every day.

The people honored their goddess, Demeter, who lovingly provided all this abundance. They held festivals in her honor, praising her for her wondrous gifts.

Demeter had a beautiful daughter, Persephone, whom she dearly loved. For Persephone she gathered the ripest figs, the choicest nuts and berries. She wove fine linen robes for her daughter, and she made her a straw hat with red ribbons. In turn, Persephone adored her mother. The two of them loved to dance together through fields of poppies, delighting in the beauty of Earth and the good people who thanked them for their gifts.

One day Persephone told her mother that she was going to bathe in a pond on the other side of the meadow. Demeter

kissed her tenderly. "I will join you after I have seen to the new fields of barley," she said. Persephone strolled away, her long hair rippling in the breeze.

When she reached a cluster of houses at the edge of the pond, Persephone heard a strange noise. It sounded like someone weeping, a rare sound in this happy land. Curious, she went around a house and through a garden, following the sound, until she came to an old olive tree. She looked up, and in the tree she saw, huddled against a branch, a ghostly figure.

"Why do you cry?" Persephone asked.

The gray wraith peered at her through bloodshot eyes. "Because this was my home, and I can no longer enter it. I am the spirit of one who lived here and died many years ago."

"You belong in the Underworld, not in the land of the living," Persephone said.

The spirit sighed mournfully. "The realm of the dead is a place of gloom and shadows, filled with restless souls. At least

here I can see the home I loved and not have to listen to sorrow."

Persephone continued on to the pond, but she couldn't forget the sad spirit. When Demeter joined her, and they had refreshed themselves and were lying on the meadow in the sun, Persephone asked, "Mother, why are the spirits in the Underworld so miserable? Is there no one to receive them, to greet them with ceremony when they arrive?"

"No one greets them. They drift and wander," her mother answered.

"Why don't you do it? The Underworld is your domain. You give birth to all living things, and all return to you."

Demeter stroked her daughter's wet and shining hair. "I'm busy here, tending to the living and caring for you."

Persephone picked a grass stem and chewed it. She was thinking, remembering the spirit's pain. At last she sat up and said, "Mother, the dead need someone to give them comfort. I'm going to the Underworld to help them."

Demeter felt an icy chill grip her heart. "No, Persephone! You can't go, it's bleak and fearful there."

"All the more reason," Persephone said. "No wonder the spirits are sad, with no one to give them a proper greeting, and no guidance. Maybe I can bring them peace."

Demeter took her daughter's hand. "Listen to the birds singing around us, smell the sweet flowers," she pleaded. "Touch the soft grass and hear the songs of the people who love us so. You don't want to give that up." Her eyes filled with tears. "And my heart would break if you were gone."

Persephone hugged her mother and kissed her cheek. "I love you, and I must do this," she said.

Demeter knew that Persephone had made up her mind. They walked together through the meadow and looked down on the fields of wheat and barley, swaying in the breeze. Demeter said, "You have a loving nature. I understand why you are going. But I will grieve as if we were mortals and you had died."

She led Persephone to a deep crack in the ground. "This is the entrance to the Underworld," she said. "It's dark and cold, and those who enter must go alone. Are you still sure you want to do this?"

"Yes," Persephone answered.

"Take this torch to light your way. Follow the stream." Persephone looked one last time on the green fields behind her, glowing in the sun. She entered the chasm. The path was narrow. Steadily she walked downward, beside the trickling stream, holding her torch high as she descended into the dark, quiet earth. Soon the path disappeared, and Persephone had to pick her way over sharp stones.

Deeper she went, and the air grew chill and dank. Her torch cast flickering shadows against the damp walls. She walked for hours in silence—even the stream of water made no noise—until she heard faint moans that sounded like all the despair and sadness the world had ever known. Never in her carefree, happy life had Persephone heard such sounds. She shuddered, and for the first time

she felt fear. Her steps faltered. "Maybe I shouldn't have come," she thought, remembering with sudden longing the warm sun and fresh air and love she had left behind.

In spite of her fear she kept on, and as she rounded a corner she found herself in an immense dark cave, where the stream flowed into a pond that reflected nothing. Beside it was a huge stone bowl filled with pomegranate seeds, the food of the dead. Persephone had entered the Underworld. Thousands of spirits, like the one she had seen in the olive tree, were shuffling about, lamenting and crying, never at rest.

Filled with pity for these lost souls, Persephone stood on a rock, raised her torch high, and said, "Hail, spirits! I am Persephone, daughter of Demeter, and I have come to help you. You have left your mortal bodies for the realm of the dead; now I will prepare you for your new place and comfort you."

The spirits nearest her looked up with glazed eyes at the radiant goddess who stood before them. She beckoned them closer,

and as each wraith approached, she embraced it. She reached into the bowl for a pomegranate seed and marked the spirit's forehead with red pomegranate juice, saying, "Your earthly life has ended, you have entered another realm. Accept the Underworld, learn wisdom, and be at peace."

Persephone went through this ceremony for every one of the thousands of spirits. It took months. Gradually the moans and lamentations slowed; the spirits were calmed.

Meanwhile, Demeter mourned for her daughter. She no longer cared about the crops and the orchards, and the plants withered and died. The people planted seeds, but nothing would grow. Demeter sat beside the chasm where she had last seen Persephone and wept, while the people went hungry.

"Demeter, we beseech you, save us!" they prayed. But she could not hear them. The world turned cold and bitter.

One day, Demeter glanced into the chasm and saw a flicker of light. It was moving. She stared, not believing her eyes. Yes!

It was Persephone, carrying her torch, walking steadily up from the depths of the Underworld.

The moment they embraced, the crops began to sprout. While mother and daughter hugged and laughed and cried and danced over the hillside, flowers budded and grass grew.

When Demeter and Persephone stopped to rest on a meadow of daisies, Persephone said, "I must return to the Underworld again, Mother. They need me there. But I will always come back."

Demeter nodded. She understood. "I will be lonely and sad when you're gone," she said. "The crops won't grow. I'll have to teach the people to store food and prepare for a time when the land will rest."

And she did. And every year, Persephone descends to the Underworld, and Earth turns cold and bleak. When the people see the first green sprouts of spring, the first crocuses and snowdrops, they rejoice. They know that Persephone has returned and Demeter is happy again.

PRONUNCIATION KEY

Abraham	AY-bruh-ham
Bodhi	BOH-dee
Buddhism	BOO-dism
Demeter	DEM-uh-ter
Gaia	GI-uh
Ganges	GAN-jeez
Hagar	HA-gahr
Herod	HAIR-ud
Inanna	ee-NAH-nah
Jasodha	jah-SOH-dah
Kaaba	KAH-bah
Khadija	kah-DEE-juh
Khumba	KOOM-bah
Lakshman	LOK-shmahn
Medina	meh-DEE-nuh
Mosque	mosk
Muhammad	moo-HAH-mud
Parvati	par-VAH-tee
Persephone	purr-SEF-uh-nee
Pharaoh	FAIR-oh
Philistines	FILL-is-teens
Ramadan	RAH-muh-don
Samaritan	suh-MAIR-i-tun
Shiva	SHEE-vah
Siddhartha Gautama	sid-AR-tha gah-TAH-ma
Suddhodana	sood-ho-DAH-nah
Sumer	SOO-mur
Synagogue	SIN-uh-gog
Tipi	TEE-pee

GLOSSARY

Allah	God of Islam, Judaism, and Christianity
Bible	The sacred book of Christianity and Judaism
Brahman	Hindu eternal spirit of the universe
Buddha	"The Awakened One"
Christ	Jesus, considered by Christians to be the Son of God
Church	Christian place of worship
Ganges	Sacred river of India
Kaaba	Arabic word for House of God
Koran	The sacred book of Islam
Mecca	City where Muhammad was born and place of pilgrimage for Muslims
Medicine Man, Medicine Woman	A healer and spiritual leader who acts as a medium between the visible world and the invisible, spirit realm
Messiah	One who will come to be a savior of the people
Moksha	Hindu state of eternal happiness, not being reborn but joining Brahman, the universal spirit
Mosque	Muslim place of worship
Nirvana	A state of supreme contentment, with no desires for worldly things, reached by meditation and right behavior
Pagan	Someone who follows the old, Earth-centered religions
Patriarch	A man who leads a group of people and may be a prophet
Prophet	One who speaks of the will of his God and foresees the future
Ramadan	Month of fasting and purification for Muslims over age thirteen
Reincarnation	Reborn in another form after death
Resurrection	Risen from the dead
Synagogue	Jewish place of worship
Vision quest	A journey alone into the wilderness to seek wisdom

FURTHER READING

Brian Wildsmith's Illustrated Bible Stories, as told by Philip Turner. Franklin Watts, 1969

The Buddha: His Life Retold, Robert Allen Mitchell. Paragon House, 1989

Coyote Stories for Children: Tales from Native America, Susan Strauss. Beyond Words
    Publishing, 1991

Coyote Was Going There: Indian Literature of the Oregon Country, ed. Jarold Ramsey.
    University of Washington Press, 1977

Earthmaker's Tales: North American Indian Stories about Earth Happenings, Gretchen
    Will Mayo. Walker Publishing Co., 1989

Hindus and Buddhists: Myths and Legends, Sister Nivedita and Ananda K. Coomaraswamy.
    Studio Editions, 1994

The Holy Bible

Human Roots: Buddhist Stories for Young Readers, translated from Chinese by Bhikshuni
    Heng Ch'ih and Upasiki T. Nicholson. Buddhist Text Translation Society, 1982

Lost Goddesses of Early Greece: A Collection of Pre-Hellenic Myths, Charlene Spretnak.
    Beacon Press, 1984

Native American Stories, told by Joseph Bruchac. Fulcrum Publishing, 1991

The Old Testament, arranged and illustrated by Marguerite de Angeli. Doubleday & Co., 1960

The Pagan Book of Days: A Guide to the Festivals, Traditions, and Sacred Days of the Year, Nigel Pennick. Destiny Books, 1992

Religions of the World, The Bookwright Press, 1986-1987 (series):

    Buddhism, John Snelling

    Hinduism, V. P. (Hemant) Kanitkar

    Islam, Al Hoad and Abdul Latif

    Judaism, Myer Domnitz

The Story-Telling Stone: Traditional Native American Myths and Tales, edited by Susan Feldmann. Dell Publishing, 1965

Teepee Tales of the American Indian, retold by Dee Brown. Holt, Rinehart and Winston, 1979

Tomie de Paola's Book of Bible Stories, Tomie de Paola. G.P. Putnam's Sons/Zondervan, 1990

The World's Religions: Understanding the Living Faiths, Peter B. Clarke, Consulting Editor. The Reader's Digest Association, 1993

ILLUSTRATION AND PHOTO CREDITS

The illustrations in this book are based on extensive research of images and symbols meaningful to each religion. Images were developed from a variety of sources: illustrations and photographs created by Design Studio Selby, copyright-free and royalty-free images, and copyrighted images and photographs from sources listed below.

p. 6 Buddha Amitabha, from Candi Borobudur, c. ninth century. Museum Nasional, Jakarta, inv. no. 226

p. 11 Seated Buddha, Central Java, from Ampel, Solo, ninth century. Museum Nasional, Jakarta, inv. no. 588

p. 13 Photo of young boy, © Ashvin Mehta

p. 15 Buddha Amitabha, from Candi Borobudur, c. ninth century. Museum Nasional, Jakarta, inv. no. 226

p. 18 "Adoration of the Shepherds with the Lamp," Rembrandt van Rijn, sketch. Foto Marburg/Art Resource, New York

pp. 20-21 "The Merciful Samaritan," Carl Julius Milde. Superstock, New York

pp. 24-25 "The Raising of Lazarus," Fra Angelico, 15th c. Museo of San Marco, Florence. Scala/Art Resource, New York

pp. 26-27 "Christ Appearing to Mary Magdalene," Aleksandr Ivanov, 19th c. State Museum, St. Petersburg. Scala/Art Resource, New York

p. 41 Four-Armed Visnu, Central Java, from Gemuruh, eighth to ninth century. Museum Nasional, Jakarta, inv. no. A31/486a

pp. 50-51 Calligraphy representing the declaration of faith. Andromeda Oxford Ltd., London

pp. 66-67 David and Goliath, Lorenzo Ghiberti, bronze relief. Porta del Paradiso, Giovanni Baptistery, Florence. Alinari/Art Resource, New York

p. 70 Red fox. Ardea, London

p. 76 Galapagos tortoise. Animals, Animals, New York

p. 87 Bronze head of a serpent from the West African kingdom of Benin, 15th to 18th century. British Museum, London

pp. 92-93 "Demeter Holding Sheaves of Wheat," Museo Nazionale delle Terme. Alinari/Art Resource, New York

p. 95 Statue of Kore (Persephone) holding an apple or pomegranate, Acropolis Museum, 510 BC. Scala/Art Resource, New York

STORY CREDITS

Two stories in this book, "The Enchanted Lake" and "The Golden Elephant," are retellings of tales that appear in *The Snow Lion's Turquoise Mane: Wisdom Tales from Tibet*, by Surya Das (Harper San Francisco, 1992). Adaptation is by permission of the author.

"Grandmother Spider Brings the Sun" and "Turtle Island" are based on stories in *Native American Stories*, told by Joseph Bruchac, from *Keepers of the Earth*, by Michael J. Caduto and Joseph Bruchac (Fulcrum Publishing, 1991). Adaptation is by permission of the author and the publisher.

"Mella and the Python Healer" is based on the story, "Mella," from *Ancient Mirrors of Womanhood* by Merlin Stone, © 1979, 1990 by Merlin Stone, adapted by permission of Beacon Press, Boston.

The myth of Demeter and Persephone is based on the research and reconstruction of the pre-Olympian version of this myth in *Lost Goddesses of Early Greece: A Collection of Pre-Hellenic Myths*, by Charlene Spretnak (Boston: Beacon Press, 1984). Adaptation here is by permission of the author.

COLOPHON

Production Notes: This book was created electronically using QuarkXpress on the Power Macintosh 6100/66AV. Typographic elements in the section lead-ins were created in Adobe Illustrator. Calligraphic elements were created by hand using a variety of brushes and papers, then scanned into Adobe Photoshop for coloring. Religious symbols in the page corners were developed by hand traditionally, made into rubber stamps, applied to highly textured paper, and scanned into Adobe Photoshop for color application to each story. Illustrations were produced using Adobe Illustrator and Adobe Photoshop on the Macintosh Quadra 840AV. Working film was produced with the PostScript language on ECRM imagesetters using Amtec film. Text material is set in Garamond Book Condensed. Headlines are set in Onyx and Garamond Book Condensed. Golden Rule statements are set in Futura Book.

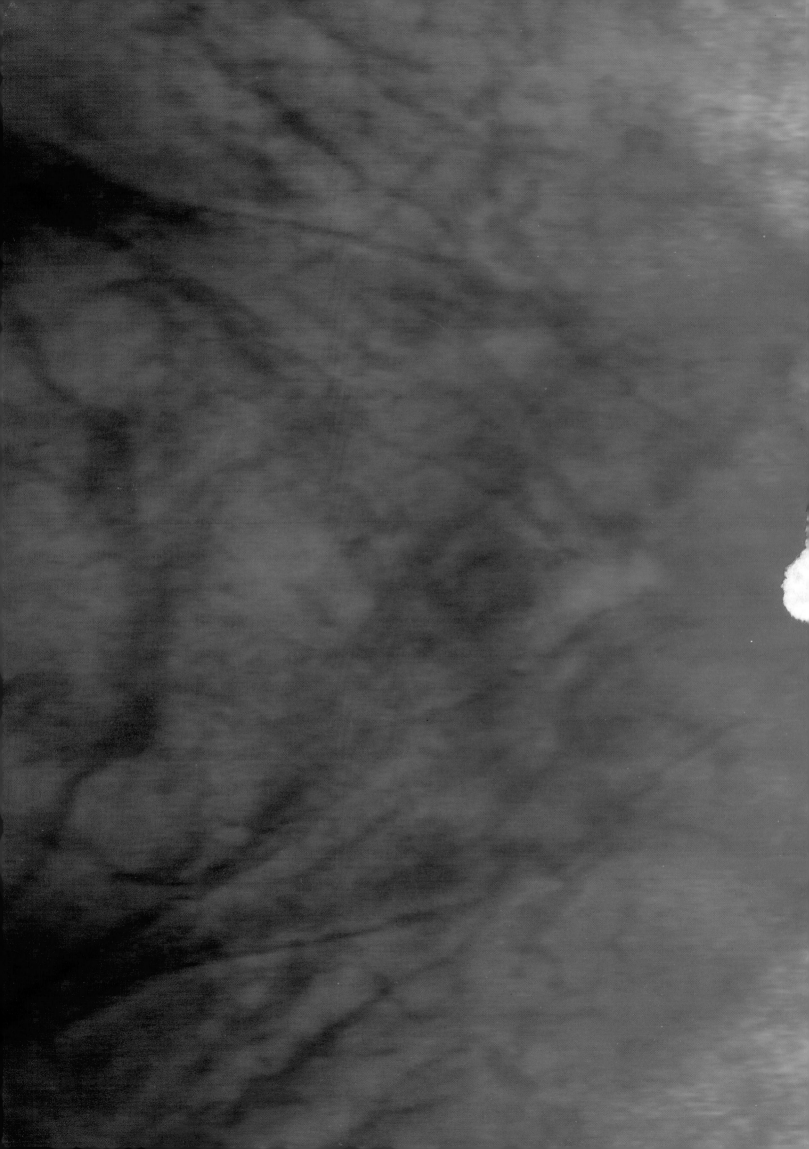

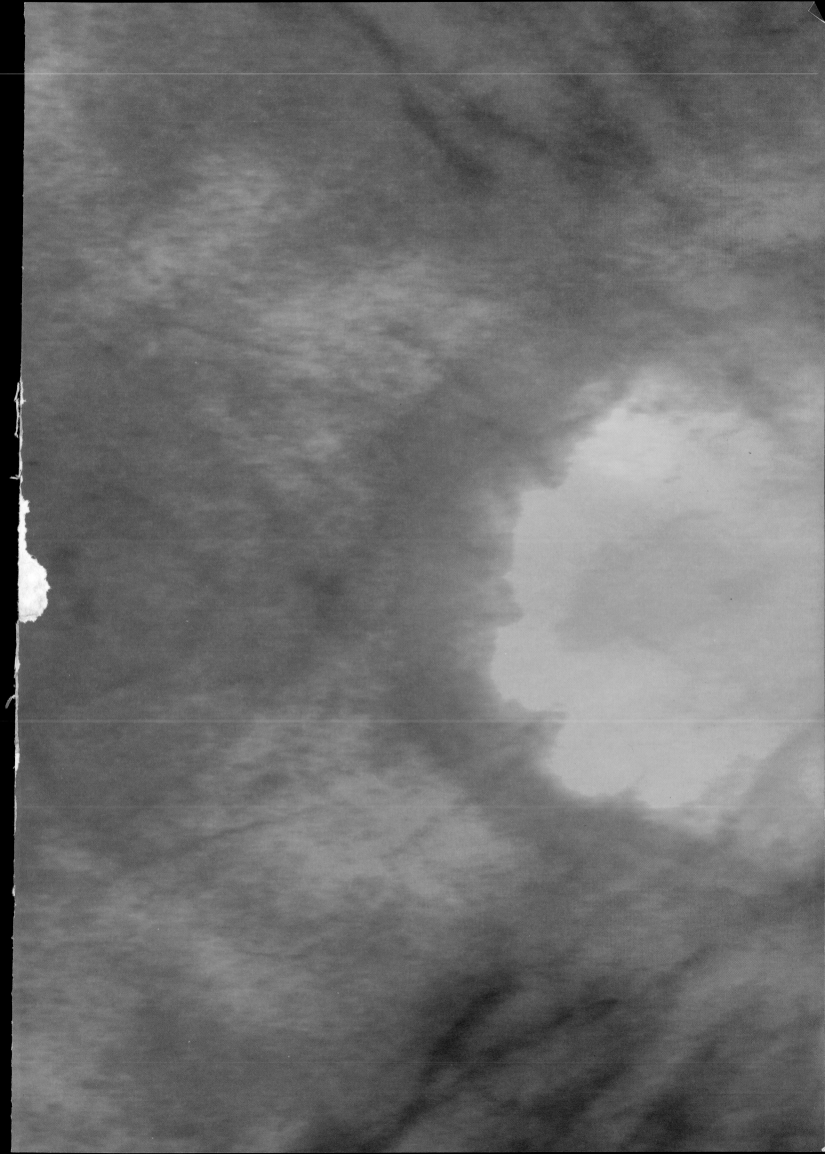